THE RIGHTS OF WOMEN IN ISLAM

Also by Haifaa A. Jawad

EURO-ARAB RELATIONS: A Study in Collective Diplomacy

THE MIDDLE EAST IN THE NEW WORLD ORDER (*editor*)

The Rights of Women in Islam

An Authentic Approach

Haifaa A. Jawad
Senior Lecturer in Middle East and Islamic Studies
Westhill College, Birmingham

First published in Great Britain 1998 by
MACMILLAN PRESS LTD
Houndmills, Basingstoke, Hampshire RG21 6XS and London
Companies and representatives throughout the world

A catalogue record for this book is available from the British Library.

ISBN 0–333–65086–7 hardcover
ISBN 0–333–73458–0 paperback

First published in the United States of America 1998 by
ST. MARTIN'S PRESS, INC.,
Scholarly and Reference Division,
175 Fifth Avenue, New York, N.Y. 10010

ISBN 0–312–21351–4

Library of Congress Cataloging-in-Publication Data
Jawad, H. A.
The rights of women in Islam : an authentic approach / Haifaa A.
Jawad.
p.   cm.
Includes bibliographical references (p.   ) and index.
ISBN 0–312–21351–4 (cloth)
1. Muslim women—Social conditions.   2. Women in Islam.
I. Title.
HQ1170.J4 1998
305.42'0917'671—dc21   97–49652
                                                                                      CIP

This book is printed on paper suitable for recycling and made from fully managed and
sustained forest sources.

10   9   8   7   6   5   4   3   2   1
07   06   05   04   03   02   01   00   99   98

Printed and bound in Great Britain by
Antony Rowe Ltd, Chippenham, Wiltshire

To my mother, a source of inspiration
and
my sister Suzanne, a deep gesture of appreciation

Contents

Introduction

As a Muslim woman born to a family which was Muslim in name but secular in practice, I never thought for a moment what Islam meant to me. It was not until fate decided to turn savagely against me, by depriving me first of my sweet sister – with whom I shared all my hopes and dreams, especially at university when we were very close – then my dear loving father, who had defied all the pressures such as honour, shame and family pride to allow me to leave Baghdad and come to Britain to pursue my dream of gaining a higher education, and then my caring brother, who stood beside me when I was on the brink of giving in to social pressure. All three departed so quickly – within the space of a few years – that I did not have enough time to grieve for them properly as individuals in their own right. The tragedy was so overwhelming that it shook me to my very foundations; my dreams in life were shattered, my hopes and ambitions vanished. I felt that I had lost my direction and began to become aware that I was going astray. It was at this particular point that I started seriously thinking about Islam. I needed refuge, peace and tranquillity, and it was Islam, especially spiritual Islam, that finally restored my faith and equilibrium.

But that conviction and equilibrium started to be disturbed by two conflicting messages: first, the attack on Islam launched by secular feminists who declared that the Islamic system is a curse on the status of women under its law, thus portraying Islam as an oppressor rather than as a liberator, and urging women to release themselves from the shackles and constraints of their religion by adopting Western secular alternatives. Second, the message conveyed by fundamentalists, who although emphasising the importance of Islam and using Islamic rhetoric, nonetheless depicted Muslim women in images totally unappealing to my inquisitive mind.

Troubled by the conflict between these views and convinced by neither, I set myself the task of embarking on a journey which would eventually lead me to discover what Islam has in store for me and my fellow Muslim women. Hence the book is in reality no more than a personal enquiry to satisfy my spiritual and theological needs: a soul-searching attempt to understand my faith (as a woman) and preserve it in a more humane form in the face of increasing secularisation and westernisation. This personal drive was then further accentuated by the realisation, especially during my years of teaching, of the widespread ignorance – on the part of both Muslim and non-Muslim women – of the proper understanding of the position of women from the Islamic perspective. Hence my urge to meet this demand.

The book aims primarily to investigate some of the issues currently affecting the situation of Muslim women. It is therefore not an exhaustive study of all issues that are of interest to Muslim women: that is certainly beyond the scope of the present study. Rather it is a personal endeavour to examine matters most immediate and sensitive to them.

The book singles out neither a particular group of women nor a specific band of countries in the Muslim region. Indeed, it deals with common issues that are of utmost concern to all Muslim women irrespective of their geographical and cultural backgrounds. The rationale behind this approach is that despite the huge diversity among Muslim countries, Islam has continued to serve as a unifying factor between them, especially when it comes to women's issues, where little has changed regarding the laws and regulations that are affecting their lives.

I would like to thank the British Academy for supporting my trips to Egypt and Yemen, without which I would not have been able to complete the study. Also, many thanks go to both Felicity Simpson Wright and Barbara Morris for typing parts of the work and showing sympathy and understanding when I needed it most. I am grateful for their support.

HAIFAA A. JAWAD

1 The Legal Status of Women in Islam

THE STATUS OF WOMEN BEFORE ISLAM

It is a well-known fact that the condition of women in general before Islam was dismal. The history of human civilisation testifies that the woman, who gives birth to man as mother, was humiliated, treated harshly and reduced to the position of being 'a maid' rather than a dignified woman.[1] Women were held in bondage to their husbands, who could keep them or divorce them at their will and pleasure.[2] Women were viewed as the embodiment of sin, misfortune, disgrace and shame, and they had no rights or position in society whatsoever. Indeed, society was confused about the very nature of women and even questioned whether God had granted them a soul.[3] Hence, they were deprived of all opportunities to develop their personalities and their individualities, and make full use of their abilities to the benefit of their society. Women in those societies were also denied all rights of inheritance and ownership. Rather, they were considered as objects of inheritance. A woman was classed not as a person but as a thing, divisible like property; she was an object of scorn and contempt.[4] These inhuman practices were prevalent at the time in most ancient societies.[5]

However, in the Arabian peninsula (the birthplace of Islam), the situation of women prior to Islam was markedly worse.[6] Women in this time of ignorance before Islam (*Jahiliyya*) were in subjugation either to their kinsmen or their husbands. They were considered a chattel to be possessed, to be bought, to be sold or to be inherited.[7] Men had absolute domination over them. They were not individuals themselves, they either belonged to their father or to their husband. The widow(s) of a man were very often inherited by his sons just like any other property. After inheriting them from their father the sons could then easily marry them.[8] Women had no independence or power over issues relating to their well-being and they were excluded from any active role in the social and political affairs of their society. It has been stated that 'at annual gatherings and fairs women were made to dance naked and poets sat around composing poems on various parts of their body and movements'.[9] In other words, they were treated as sex objects with no respect at all for their dignity.

Women in pre-Islamic Arab times were also considered to be a heavy burden on the family. The birth of the daughter was embarrassing for the father, who considered it a disgrace and a matter of shame. Therefore, the Arabs of that time practised widely 'female infanticide': burying their female child alive. This custom was common among the Arabs and it was even viewed as a generous act.[10] The Quran described the mentality of ignorance underlying such a practice as such: 'When the birth of a girl is announced to one of them, his face grows dark and he is filled with inward gloom. Because of the bad news, he hides himself from men: should he keep her with disgrace or bury her under the dust? How ill they judge!'.[11] 'When the sun is folded up; when the stars fall down and the mountains are blown away; when camels big with their young are left untended and the wild beasts are brought together; when the seas are burning and men's souls are reunited (with their bodies); when the infant girl, buried alive, is asked for what crime she was slain; when the records of men's deeds are laid open and heaven is stripped bare; when Hell burns fiercely and Paradise is brought near: then each soul shall know what it has done'.[12]

One of the social reasons for such an attitude was that, in pre-Islamic times, there were often inter-tribal blood feuds, which demanded male members to defend their tribes. Hence men were in much greater demand than women. In addition, in the tribal conflict, the enemy always aimed at capturing women and taking them as prisoners so that they could collect heavy ransoms. Failing to do so, they would keep them as slaves. In both cases women were considered a liability to their own tribes. For if they paid ransom, they would lose money, if not, then the chastity of their women as well as their honour were at stake.[13] 'The Arabs did not welcome the birth of a baby girl, and this was so because of the nature of their society. Wars and invasions never ceased and taking revenge never stopped. All these things depended on the male, but a woman was unable to do any of these tasks, in addition to it, she was the desired loot for (the) service (of the enemy) in the eyes of the enemy, or she was for his entertainment'.[14] For these reasons, the Arabs believed that their own daughters constituted a heavy burden on them and the easiest way to get rid of them was to kill them immediately after they were born.[15]

Moreover, men in the *Jahiliyya* society enjoyed an absolute right over women in matters related to marriage and divorce. He, the man, had unlimited rights of marriage and divorce. He could take as many wives as he wished and could discard a wife at will.[16] The idea of a fixed institution of marriage was absent from the pre-Islamic era. There were only different kinds of sexual union[17] which were characterised by the looseness of marriage bonds and the lack of any defined legal system: 'If one takes into consideration the preceding facts in conjunction with other factors such as the absence of any contract or legal guardian, the exclusion of the wife from her husband's inheritance, the easy methods of divorce, the lack of a period of seclusion after divorce and widowhood – the *idda* (waiting time) – the conclusion must be reached that there was no fixed institution of marriage and that marriage ties were in no sense regarded as binding'.[18] The result was that a man was at liberty to contract as many marriages as he wished; al-Tabari mentions that men in Arabia before Islam used to marry four, five, six, or even ten women simultaneously and nobody could ever stop them from marrying more than that[19] 'Before Muhammad, the capacity of the Arab's purse would appear to have provided the only limitation to the number of his wives, and though there were established conventions about the status of the women he married, there were neither conventions nor laws to dictate to him how many they should be'.[20] When Islam emerged, the issue of marriage was regulated. It encouraged men to have one wife, but reluctantly allowed them to have up to four wives under special circumstances.[21] Men before Islam also used to force their women, especially their slave girls, into prostitution (*Zina*).[22]

With regard to divorce, there was no formula for severing the marriage relationship. The husband, in general, enjoyed absolute power over the divorce issue[23] and this led to constant abuses. As there was no check on the powers of the husband to dissolve the marriage tie, Arab men used to divorce their women very often and for any reason,[24] even if it was a trivial one such as, for example, speaking highly of their family or tribes. However, the most obvious ones mentioned by the historians of the *Jahiliyya* were: the man could not find the love he was expecting in his wife; the couple were unable to establish friendship and intimacy or a man thought that he was marrying a young and beautiful woman who turned out to be otherwise.[25] The pagan Arabs also used to revoke the divorce and resume the marital relationship. A man, for example, would pronounce the formula 'I divorce you'[26] many times and then take his wife back; he could then divorce her again and yet could still take her back. When women were divorced or widowed there was no fixed period[27] for *idda*. Some women had to wait for a year before they would be able to re-marry, others contracted marriages immediately after the separation.[28] Divorced women had no right to claim for maintenance, men were exempted from any financial responsibility and endured no legal punishment for their actions.[29] This inhuman treatment had contributed to the degradation of womanhood insofar as the woman herself believed that she should not be more than a servile and submissive creature, and had no right to expect any respect and honour in the world. Such a deplorable situation illustrated that the rights and the liberties of women in those ancient societies were not only trampled upon, but were entirely denied them.

It must be stressed that some scholars have argued that women in pre-Islamic Arabia had some rights, citing the case of Khadija, the Prophet's first wife, who was a highly successful business-woman. Our response is that Khadija was an exception, one among a small elite of that society, and we believe that her case does not genuinely reflect the general condition of women in that society, which was one of subjugation. This view is shared by B. Stowasser[30] who writes 'we hear of publicly visible, independently wealthy women who are active in their own right. The best-known example here is, of course, Khadija, Muhammad's first wife … (but) aside from such rare figures of public visibility, involvement and independence as Khadija, the majority of pre-Islamic urban women appear to have lived in a male-dominated society in which their status was low and their rights were negligible. Most women were subjugated to male domination, either that of a male relative, or that of the husband. The men's rights over their women were as their rights over any property. This seems to have been so not only in marriages by capture, where the captured woman was completely under the authority of her captor, but also in marriages by purchase or contract. Here, the suitor paid a sum of money (the *mahr*) to the guardian of the bride-to-be (and possibly another sum, the *sadaq*, to the woman herself),-thereby purchasing her and making her his exclusive property. The marriage contract, in other words, was a contract between husband and guardian, with the bride the sales object. Furthermore, neither conventions nor laws seem to have existed to put a limit to the number of wives that a man could have simultaneously, so that the only restrictive considerations were economic ones. As to divorce in the *Jahiliyya*, it was a matter entirely up to the will of the husband who, having purchased his wife, could discharge his total obligation to her by payment of any portion of the *mahr* that might remain due to her father or guardian, and be rid of her by pronouncement of the formula of dismissal. This formula, pronounced three times, was effective instantly. Finally, there is some indication that women in pre-Islamic Arabia were not allowed the holding, or in any case the uncontrolled disposal, of their possessions'.[31]

WOMEN IN ISLAM

With the advent of Islam, the position of women was radically redefined. Firstly, it prohibited the practice of 'female infanticide' and restored the birth rights of women.[32] Hence Islam elevated them to the status of being as worthy of human dignity as were men. Both men and women were henceforth to be regarded as equal in humanity. The Quran says 'Allah created you from a single soul, and from the same soul created his mate'.[33] It also says 'O mankind, we created you all from a male and female, and made you into races and tribes, that you may know one another. Surely the noblest among you in the sight of God is the most God fearing of you'.[34] The prophet is reported to have said 'All people are equal, as equal as the teeth of a comb. There is no claim of merit of an Arab over a non-Arab, or of a white over a black person, or of a male over a female. Only God-fearing people merit a preference with God'.[35]

In relation to the absolute, woman is equal to man in all essential rights and duties; God makes no distinction between man and woman. They are to be equally rewarded or punished for their deeds.[36] The Quran says: 'Their Lord answers them, saying: I will deny no man or woman among you the reward of their labours. You are the offspring of one another'.[37] 'For Muslim men and women, for believing men and women; for devout men and women; for men and women who are patient; for men and women who humble themselves; for men and women who give charity; for men and women who fast; for men and women who guard their chastity; for men and women who remember Allah much – for them all has God prepared forgiveness and a great reward'.[38] 'We shall reward the steadfast according to their noblest deeds. Be they men or women, those that embrace the faith and do what is right We will surely grant a happy life; We shall reward them according to their noblest actions'.[39] And again 'The true believers, both men and women, are friends to each other. They enjoin what is just and forbid what is evil; they attend to their prayers and pay the alms-tax and obey Allah and His Apostle. On these Allah will have mercy. He is Mighty, Wise. Allah has promised the men and women who believe in Him gardens watered by running streams, in which they shall abide forever. He has promised them goodly mansions in the gardens of Eden. And what is more, they shall have greater favour from Allah. That is the supreme triumph'.[40] Furthermore, *Surah* 40 (the Forgiving one) verse 40:30 'O my people, the life of this world is nothing but a (passing) comfort, but the life to come is an everlasting mansion. Those that do evil shall be rewarded with like evil; but those that have faith and do good works, both men and women, shall enter the Gardens of Paradise and receive blessings without number'.[41] In terms of moral responsibility, both men and women are equally accountable for their actions. For example, the Quran decrees that the same punishment has to be applied on the thieving men as well as the thieving women.[42] Also, both the adulterer and the adulteress have to suffer the same punishment.[43] In fact, in a situation where the husband accuses his wife of committing adultery, her oath weighs more heavily than his accusation and hence Islamic law would work in her favour.[44]

To rehabilitate the status of women in society, Islam denounced the old myth of Eve as temptress and source of evil, as the cause of original sin and the fall of humankind.[45] According to the Quran the woman is not responsible for Adam's first mistake: both were equally wrong in disobeying God. Both asked for forgiveness and both were forgiven. Indeed in one verse Adam was portrayed as solely responsible for the whole episode: 'But Satan made them slip from it and caused them to depart from that in which they had been. Go hence, We said, and be enemies to each other. The earth will for a while provide your dwelling-place and sustenance. Then Adam received commandments from his Lord, and his Lord relented towards him. He is the Forgiving One, the Merciful'.[46] 'To Adam He said: Dwell with your wife in Paradise, and eat from whatever you please; but never approach this tree or you shall both become transgressors. But the devil tempted them, so that he might reveal to them that which had been hidden from them of their shame. He said: your Lord has forbidden you to approach this tree only to prevent you from becoming angels or immortals. Then he swore to them that he would give them friendly counsel. Thus he cunningly seduced them. And when they had eaten of the tree, their shame became visible to them, and they both covered themselves with the leaves of the garden. Their Lord called out to them, saying: did I not forbid you to approach that tree, and did I not warn you that the devil was your sworn enemy? They replied: Lord we have wronged ourselves. Pardon us and have mercy on us, or we shall surely be among the lost. He said: Go hence, and may your descendants be enemies to each other. The earth will for a while provide your sustenance and dwelling-place.[47] There you shall live and there you shall die, and thence you shall be raised to life'.[48] 'But Satan whispered to him, saying: shall I show you the Tree of Immorality and a kingdom which never decays?.... Thus Adam disobeyed his Lord and went astray. Then his Lord had mercy on him; He relented towards him and rightly guided him'.[49]

Islam also changed the mentality of both men and women and created a new relationship between them based on respect and mutual understanding; taking care of the woman and respecting her were also emphasised.[50] The status of women was also raised in Islam by granting her the legal right to enter into contracts, to run a business, and to possess property independently from her husband or any kinsmen.[51] From the beginning, Islam stressed that women, as half of the society, should be offered all opportunities which could enable them to develop their natural abilities, so that they might participate effectively in the development of society. It also emphasised that women should be allowed to attain to the highest ranks of progress materially, intellectually and spiritually.

It is within this context that Islam has granted women broad social, political and economic rights, education and training rights and work opportunity rights. To protect these rights from being abused by men, Islam provided firm legal safeguards.[52] In theory, therefore, a Muslim woman is entitled to the following.

(1) *The Right of Independent Ownership.* This involves the right to manage her own money and property independently. She is at liberty to buy, sell, mortgage, lease, borrow or lend, and sign contracts and legal documents. Also, she can donate her money, act as a trustee and set up a business or company.[53] 'For men is a portion of what they earn, and for women is a portion of what they earn. Ask Allah for His grace. Allah has knowledge of all things'.[54] This right cannot be altered whether she is single or married. When she is married, she enjoys a free hand over the dower while she is married and after divorce.[55] This independent economic position is based on Quranic principles, especially the teaching of *Zakat*, which encourages women to own, invest, save and distribute their earnings and savings according to their discretion. It also acknowledges and enforces the right of women to participate in various economic activities.[56]

(2) *The Right to Marry Whom She Likes, and to End an Unsuccessful Marriage.* Islam regards marriage as a meritorious institution and attaches great importance to its well-being. Marriage in Islam is a union between two consenting adults. Its aims are to perpetuate human life and achieve spiritual and emotional harmony.[57] The Quran says[58] 'And of His signs is that He created you from dust and behold: you became men and multiplied throughout the earth. And of His signs is that He gave you wives from among yourselves, that you might live in tranquillity with them, and put love and kindness in your hearts. Surely there are signs in this for thinking people'.[59] Also, the Prophet is reported to have said 'women are the twin halves of men'.[60] Therefore, the consent of the two partners is essential to start a happy and stable family. Hence Islam is against the idea of forcing women to marry against their wishes. On the contrary, it encourages women to choose their spouses. According to the Prophet, 'A widow (or divorcee) is not to be married before her consent is sought' and 'No virgin girl is to marry without first consulting her, and her approval is her keeping silent'.[61] This freedom to choose her partner is guaranteed by the law which insists that the dowry has to be paid to the bride and not to the parents. The Prophet emphasised that although parents were to be

consulted and obeyed, the fact remained that the woman's individuality and independence had to be recognised and respected. Hence the marriage contract has to reflect the interests of the woman in the first instance and be designed to meet her specific needs. The woman has to express her desire and impose conditions if necessary to secure her position.[62] A Muslim woman, therefore, cannot be forced to enter into marriage without her agreement; indeed she has the right to revoke a marriage to which she did not agree in the first place. The Prophet set a precedent for Muslim women when he invalidated marriages which were imposed on daughters by their parents. Let us see the Prophet's response when he heard that a girl was forced by her father to marry against her will: Ibn Abbas reported that a girl came to the Prophet complaining that her father had forced her to marry against her wishes. Upon hearing the story the Prophet granted her the choice between accepting the marriage or invalidating it. Also, Khaddam, Khansa's father forced her to marry a man she did not like; soon afterwards she complained to the Prophet. The Prophet respected her will to marry a man of her choice, so, he revoked the marriage and freed Khansa from her marital obligation.[63]

As a woman has the right to have a say on issues concerning her own marriage, equally she has the right to initiate divorce if the partnership proves to be unsuccessful. If the marriage contract states that she has the right to divorce her husband, she could divorce him instantly; otherwise, she would have to resort to the court to dissolve the marital relationship. Overall, the Quranic legislation concerning divorce allows time for reflection and insists on kind treatment of the woman. For example, whilst in pre-Islamic times a woman could easily be repudiated and thrown out by her husband, under the Quranic legislation he is no longer allowed to do so. If divorce takes place, the husband has to pay her back the deferred dowry and a reasonable sum of money as maintenance.[64] He has to support her throughout the *idda* period (three months and ten days) to determine whether she is pregnant. If so he is legally obliged to support her until she delivers and nurses the baby to a certain age.[65]

(3) *The Right to Education.* Both the Quran and the Sunnah advocate the rights of women and men equally to seek knowledge. The Quran commands all Muslims to exert effort in the pursuit of knowledge irrespective of their sex. It constantly encourages Muslims to read, think, contemplate and learn from the signs of Allah in nature: 'Are the wise and the ignorant equal? Truly, none will take heed but men of understanding'.[66] 'Allah will raise to high ranks those that have faith and knowledge among you. He is cognizant of all your actions'.[67] 'Say: Lord, increase me in knowledge'.[68] The Prophet moreover encouraged education for both males and females

and even ordered that slave girls should be educated. He made it clear that seeking knowledge was a matter of religious duty binding upon every Muslim man and woman. His teachings were widely sought by both sexes and at the time of his death it was reported that there were many women scholars.[69] So in Islam there can be no restriction of knowledge to one sex at the expense of the other. Today, however, family circumstances, together with the traditions and customs of specific Muslim countries, may work to the detriment of the girl, in terms of depriving her of education, for reasons which have nothing to do with Islam.[70]

(4) *The Right to Keep Her Own Identity.* A woman in Islam has always been entitled, by law, to keep her family name and not take her husband's name. Therefore, she is always known by her family's name as an indication of her individuality and her own identity. So, in Islam, there is no process of changing the names of women be they married, divorced or widowed.

(5) *The Right to Sexual Pleasure.* In Islam lawful sex (that is, within the context of a marriage relationship) has always been held in high esteem and regarded as an act of religious devotion for which rewards in the here-after are acknowledged. It is meant to lead to a healthy way of human reproduction, release tensions, meet natural and psychological needs and strengthen the marriage ties between spouses. Here are some *Hadiths* that have been attributed to the Prophet in this regard: 'When a husband and his wife look at each other lovingly, God will look at them with His merci-ful eye. When they hold hands their sins will fall away from between their fingers. When they engage in coitus they will be surrounded by prayerful angels. For every sensation of their delight there is a counterpart of reward for them in paradise as huge as a mountain. If the wife conceives, she will have the rewards of a worshipper who is constantly engaged in prayers, fasting and in the struggle in the way of God. When she delivers a child, only God knows the magnitude of the rewards stored for the parents in paradise'. 'Once a companion having heard the Prophet praising coitus with one's wife as a charitable act for which a Divine reward was to be awaited, retorted: "O you, the Messenger of God. Would a person satisfy his lust and anticipate Divine reward for it?" The Prophet said, "would he be punished if he (or she) does so with the wrong partner? In the same way, fulfillment of sensual satisfaction in the legitimate way shall be rewarded"'.[71] Contrary to the present situation in which talk about legiti-mate sex has disappeared from religious thinking and writing and has become a matter of shame and stigma which ought to be suppressed, early Muslim scholars were fascinated by the idea and were quite open about it.

They wrote chapters on the subject in which they elaborated on issues such as the anatomy of sex, the religious merits of lawful sexual activities, the intimate theme of coitus, its initial foreplay and its proper conclusion. They cautioned against an abrupt coitus and crude departure at the end of the act. Instead they advised an initial gentle approach and a slow courteous departure. Moreover, they emphasised the fact that the husband should be considerate and gentle, never too rough and that he should prolong sufficiently for his wife to attain climax. A wife is encouraged to take the initiative and not be content with the role of being submissive.[72] In their writings those early Muslim scholars were guided by the following traditions which have been attributed to the Prophet: 'It is a rude manner of a man to proceed to have intercourse with his wife without first playing with her'. 'Let not any of you fall upon his wife in the manner a male animal suddenly jumps upon his female partner. Let there be a messenger (to go) between them' (said the prophet). He was then asked: What is the Messenger, 'O you Messenger of God?' He said: 'kissing and endearing speech'. 'When one of you copulates with his wife, let him not rush away from her, having attained his own climax, until she is satisfied'. 'Wash your clothes, brush your teeth. Trim your hair. Keep always clean and tidy. A nation before you neglected themselves, thereby driving their women into adultery'. It is a vice in a man 'to assault his unprepared wife, seeking to satisfy his own lust and leaving her before she could achieve her own fulfilment'.[73] Accordingly, if a woman feels that she is not sexually satisfied or her husband is impotent she has the right to seek divorce.

(6) *The Right to Inheritance.* The Quran has allotted a share for the woman in the inheritance of her parents and kinsmen. Her share is guaranteed by law and it is completely hers. No one can have any claim on it. The Quran says 'Men shall have a share in what their parents and kinsmen leave; and women shall have a share in what their parents and kinsmen leave; whether it be little or much, it is legally theirs'.[74] However, very often in reality the culture of specific Muslim countries subject women to social pressure to renounce their shares to the immediate male members of the family. This constitutes a gross violation of the Quranic verses concerning inheritance.

(7) *The Right of Election and Nomination to Political Offices and Participation in Public Affairs.* Islam encourages women to be active politically and to be involved in decision-making. In fact Islam is the only religion which acknowledges a political role for women.[75] In early Islam women were given every opportunity to express themselves, to argue,[76] and to speak their mind in public.[77] They led delegations,[78] mediated and granted refuge and protection.[79] Their judgements on political matters

were highly valued and respected and they exercised great influence in shaping their own societies. Aisha and Umm Salama (the wives of the prophet) are clear cases in point. Umm Salama was a shrewd political adviser to the Prophet and very often acted as *imam* for women. Aisha, on the other hand, played a dominant part in the political arena she lived in. She lodged complaints, criticised the policies of the rulers and led opposition groups. Together with Umm Salama she played a crucial role in compiling the traditions of the Prophet, which are considered one of the main sources of Islamic Jurisprudence. For a considerable time she acted as a judge correcting and guiding the leaders of her time.

(8) *The Right to Respect.* Islam regards women to be equal to men as human beings; hence it emphasises mutual understanding and respect between the two sexes. From the Islamic viewpoint, women as human beings and as half of the society should be treated with care, tenderness and affection. Indeed, the Prophet insisted on kind and gentle treatment of women and demonstrated this not only through his attitude towards his wives but also in his teachings to his followers. He constantly encouraged them to be kind, civil and considerate when dealing with women: 'The more civil and kind a Muslim is to his woman whether wife, daughter or sister the more perfect in faith he is' he declared.[80] In his farewell pilgrimage he delivered a famous speech (*Khutba*) on the Mount of Mercy at Arafat in which he reminded his followers of their duty towards women and ordered them to be kind and respectful to them. He said 'Fear Allah regarding women. Verily you have married them with the trust of Allah, and made their bodies lawful with the word of Allah. You have got (rights) over them, and they have got (rights) over you'.[81]

So, from the authentic Islamic perspective, a woman is 'an individual worthy of dignity and respect, an independent human being, a social person, a legal person, a responsible agent, a free citizen, a servant of God, and a talented person, endowed, like a male person, with heart, soul and intellect; and has a fundamental equal right to exercise her abilities in all areas of human activities'.[82]

Within the context of family ties, the legal status of Muslim women can be considered at different stages:

(1) *As a Daughter:* Before the advent of Islam, daughters were very disfavoured and considered to be social and economic liabilities. Boys, on the other hand were favoured and sought after (one may add that even today in some Muslim countries boys are considered preferable to girls). Islam stopped such cruelties and insisted on equal treatment between the two

sexes. The Prophet asserted the right of a female child to be treated on an equal footing with her brother. He urged parents not to make any differences between the children and to be kind to them, particularly young girls. Here are a few *Hadiths* in which he encouraged Muslims to be gentle and caring to their daughters: 'If a daughter is born to a man and he brings her up affectionately, shows her no disrespect and treats her in the same manner as he treats his sons, the Lord will reward him with paradise'. 'Girls are models of affection and sympathy and a blessing to the family. If a person has one daughter, God will screen him from the fire of the hell owing to his daughter; if he has two daughters, God will admit him to paradise; if he has three daughters, God will exempt him from the obligations of charity and Jihad'. 'If a person has three daughters whom he provides for and brings up, God will surely reward him with paradise'. 'If a daughter is born to a person and he brings her up, gives her a good education and trains her in the arts of life, 1 shall myself stand between him and hell fire'.[83] Not content with moral exhortations which aimed at ensuring the equal rights of young girls, the prophet himself set an example for Muslims to follow. He treated his four daughters with parental love and compassion.[84] He played with them, looked after them and carried them when they were young. When they were grown up and got married, he continued to care for their well- being. Fatima, the youngest, and the only one who survived her father, was very close to him, and often he used to visit her, invite her with her family to a meal with him, and would take her warmly between his arms and offer her his seat. He used to say that Fatima was 'A part of me; who wrongs her wrongs me and who pleases her pleases me'.[85]

(2) *As a Mother*: Women as mothers enjoy great respect and affection. The Quran advises Muslims to show love, gratitude and consideration for parents, particularly mothers. It says 'And We enjoined man (to show kindness) to his parents, for weakness after weakness his mother bears him and he is not weaned before he is two years of age. We said: Give thanks to Me and to your parents. To Me shall all things return'.[86] 'your Lord has enjoined you to worship none but Him, and to show kindness to your parents. If either or both of them attain old age with you, show them no sign of impatience, nor rebuke them; but speak to them kind words. Treat them with humility and tenderness and say: Lord be merciful to them. They nursed me when 1 was an infant'.[87] The prophet taught his followers how to look after their mothers and obey them. Disobeying parents, especially mothers, is one of the greatest of all sins. The Prophet is reported to have said the following *Hadiths* regarding mothers:[88] 'Do not leave your mother unless she gives you permission or death takes her, because that is the greatest (deed) for your reward'. 'Whoever kissed his

mother between the eyes is protected from the fire'. 'If l became aware of my parents, or one of them, and l had begun the *Isha* prayer and recited *Surat al-Fatihah*; then, my mother called me: O Muhammad! l would have answered her'. 'Verily Allah has forbidden rudeness to mothers'.[89]

(3) *As a Sister*: A Muslim is required to have a close relationship with relatives, especially the immediate members of the family such as sisters, cousins, aunts, and so on. The Prophet instructed his followers to visit them, be kind to them and to help them if they needed help. He said 'He is not of me who severs or breaks the ties of kinship'.[90] Within this context, the sister occupies a special position. She is to be treated with care, respect and due consideration. The Prophet did not have a sister but he did have female cousins and relatives whom he used to welcome properly and treat tenderly and kindly. Once he stated, 'whoever is ... taking charge of two sisters, and treats them well and patiently, he and l shall be in paradise'.[91]

(4) *As a Wife*: Good treatment of wives is strongly emphasised both in the Quran and the Sunnah. The Quran describes the relationship between the husband and wife as follows: 'they (your wives) are an apparel to you and you are an apparel to them'.[92] The Prophet laid great stress upon good treatment of a wife. He said 'The best of you are they who behave best to their wives'. 'A Muslim must not hate his wife, and if he be displeased with one bad quality in her, let him be pleased with one that is good'.[93] Apart from these recommendations,[94] the Prophet set a good example as the model husband who treated his wives with loving compassion and due consideration. He dealt with them on an equal footing, devoted a night to each in turn, helped them with the housework, mended his own clothes, shared with them the ups and downs of life, listened to their opinions and gave them the chance to develop their own individuality, independence and talents. For example, Sauda developed her skill in fine leather work and earned a good income therefrom; Zaynab was very much active in charitable works to the extent that she was renowned as 'the mother of the poor';[95] Umm Salama, bright and clever, acted as a political adviser to the Prophet, while Aisha, the youngest and wittiest, was regarded as a judge, and was very often consulted on religious affairs in the absence of her husband. The Prophet's example was followed by the early generations who were very much impressed by his attitude toward his wives.[96]

In a nutshell, then, Islam 'came to grant woman her rightful place in the society of man, raising her above the position of goods and chattels and (acknowledging her as) a respectful entity and a personality unto herself.

She was considered an independent social and economic unit functioning in her own individual right, if she so desired. For the first time she was given the right to education, the right to hold property in her own name, the right of inheritance, and above all, the right to vote and pray'.[97]

Under this bill of rights women, under the leadership of Muhammad, enjoyed full freedom to develop their individuality and personality and to take part in shaping their own society. Moreover, women took advantage of the liberty offered to them: they participated effectively in public life; took part in prayers at the mosque together with the men; acted as *imams* for women (and sometimes for both sexes in their household); joined their colleagues in military expeditions; granted protection in war and asylum to fugitives; devoted themselves to the study of theology, the Quran and the traditions; travelled widely, and moved freely and mixed with men with self-respect and dignity.[98]

However, this situation did not last long; with the death of Muhammad and the transformation of the early Islamic community into an empire, women's rights steadily underwent erosion. Slowly but surely the rights granted them and enjoyed during the time of Muhammad were taken away. They were discouraged from participating in public affairs; prevented from visiting the mosques; denied any opportunity to express their opinions; barred from developing their intellectual abilities; restricted in their movements and confined to their four walls at home. Gradually the bright picture of the free, courageous, independent, self-respecting and respected Muslim woman was replaced with that of secluded, lazy, ignorant and passive woman who had no role or impact on her own affairs let alone on society as a whole. The situation became worse with the political disintegration and the subsequent social demoralisation and the penetration of foreign ideas and customs.[99] This depressed situation has persisted more or less until the present day in various shapes and forms throughout the Muslim world. It is, therefore, hardly untrue to state that women in much of the Muslim world have long been subjected to both cultural and political oppression. While men have equally suffered from the latter, women generally have had to pay a double price: culturally as well as politically. It has long been argued that Islam liberated Muslim women by granting them full rights as citizens. It is certainly true that Islamic precepts offer women a full and positive role in society as well as personal rights, which should, in theory, leave little to be desired. The question arises, however, as to whether the reality of Muslim women's lives reflects the theory. To what extent have Muslim women been able to enjoy the rights the *Sharia* (Islamic Law) grants them without being subjected to strong countervailing social pressure?

In the contemporary Muslim world, everything has been taken out of its context. Women's rights are no exception. Women have in many cases been deprived even of the basic human rights advocated by Islam itself. Forced marriages, arbitrary divorces, female mutilations and other abuses are sadly common in the Muslim world, as are restrictions on women's education and on their role in the labour force. In order to better their position as dignified human beings we need to address these and other issues in the light of the contemporary situation. I am not suggesting that we should abandon the tradition – only those aspects of cultural oppression that go under the name of tradition; nor am I arguing for an acceptance of the rigid interpretation of the role of Muslim women as it has been defined in traditional societies. Rather, it is a question of appraising the reality of their suffering in the light of the authentic principles of justice and fairness, revealed in the Quran and practised in the early days of Islam by the Prophet and his Companions.

2 Islam and Women's Education*

One of the most important rights granted to women by Islam is the right to education. To start to examine this issue, we should ask some questions. What is the position of Islam in relation to education in general and women's education in particular? What are their opportunities in relation to employment? Finally, what is the position of women in the contemporary period in the light of the authentic approach to these issues, as expressed both in the philosophy and in the practices of early Islam?

ISLAM AND EDUCATION

Knowledge and education are highly emphasised in Islam. Both are integral parts of the Islamic religion. Islam encourages its followers to enlighten themselves with the knowledge of their religion as well as other branches of knowledge. It holds the person who seeks knowledge in high esteem and has exalted his position.[1] In reality, the entire aim of the Divine revelation and the sending of prophets to humankind has been stressed in the Quran as the communication of knowledge. The Book says: 'The Prophet recites unto people God's revelation; causes them to grow and imparts to them knowledge, and wisdom'.[2] The Divine desires every believer to be well educated in religion, to possess wisdom and broad intellectual knowledge.[3] Hence the purpose of raising a prophet in a nation is to teach and to impart knowledge. The Prophet said 'I have been raised up as a teacher'.[4] The Quran is full of verses which praise learned people, encourage original thinking and personal investigation and denounce unimaginative imitation. It also emphasises the importance of the study of nature and its laws. According to the Quran, learning is an unending process and the entire universe is made subservient to man, the agent of God, who has to abide by the truth and not by narrow notions of hereditary customs and beliefs.[5] 'We did not create the heavens and the earth, and all between them merely in sport. We created them only for just ends, but most of mankind do not understand'.[6] The verses in the

* Some of the material in this chapter has been previously published in Haifaa A. Jawad, *The Education of Women in Islam*, Gulf Center for Strategic Studies, London, 1991, reproduced by kind permission of the publisher.

Quran which enjoin people to learn and observe nature outnumber all those related to prayer, fasting, and pilgrimage put together.[7] Indeed, the first verse of the Quran was a command to the Prophet to read (*Iqra*): 'Read! In the name of your Lord Who created, created man from clots of congealed blood. Read! Your Lord is the Most Bountiful One, Who taught by the pen, taught man what he did not know'.[8] Here the Prophet was told to learn, study and understand in the name of God, who, by His grace, has given man the ability to write with the pen, so that he could circulate knowledge broadly and preserve his cultural heritage generation after generation.[9] Other Quranic verses which advocate knowledge and learning are the following: 'Allah will raise to high ranks those that have faith and knowledge among you. He is cognizant of all your actions'.[10] 'Are the wise and the ignorant equal?'.[11] 'Say: Lord, increase me in knowledge'.[12]

In the *Hadith* literature, knowledge is highly appreciated and encouraged also. The Prophet Muhammad always emphasised the importance of knowledge to his followers and encouraged them to seek it. Learned people are regarded as the inheritors of the prophetic wisdom. In this connection, the following *Hadiths* can be quoted: 'The prophets leave knowledge as their inheritance. The learned ones inherit this great fortune'. 'Search for knowledge though it be in China'. The Prophet also said 'He who goes forth in search of knowledge, is in the way of Allah till he returns'.[13] To rise up at dawn and learn a section of knowledge is better than to pray one hundred rak'at. 'To be present in an assembly with a learned man is better than praying one thousand rak'at'. 'To listen to the instructions of science and learning for one hour is more meritorious than attending the funerals of a thousand martyrs'. 'One hour's meditation on the work of the Creator in a devout spirit is better than seventy years of prayer'. The Prophet was asked: 'O Messenger of God, is it better than the reading of the Quran?'. He replied: 'What benefit does the Quran give except through knowledge'.[14] 'There are only two persons that one is permitted to envy: the one to whom God has given riches and who has the courage to spend his means for the cause of truth; and the one to whom God has given wisdom and who applies it for the benefit of mankind and shares it with his fellows'.[15]

It was in accordance with this Quranic guidance and the prophetic instructions that the Muslims started, from the very beginning, to seek knowledge. Studies were conducted in the Mosques, circles of discussion (*halaqat*) were set up; and teachers were simultaneously students learning from their superiors and, in their turn, teaching their own students.[16] Education was considered a matter of religious duty – a manifestation of the Muslim's submission to the will of Allah and an act of piety which could lead to a deeper knowledge of the Creator – the One.[17] Hence we find that all members of society participated in that process. Since education was free of charge, opportunities were available to everybody, rich or poor alike. The Prophet said 'Treat equally poor and rich students who sit before you for the acquisition of knowledge'.[18] Gifted students were helped and highly encouraged to continue their education, so that they would be able to fulfill their aspirations. Moreover, the seeking of knowledge was not circumscribed by age limitations; the Prophet said 'Seek knowledge from the cradle to the grave'. Therefore, we find that the companions of the Prophet sought knowledge even when they were at an advanced age.[19] Also, there was considerable academic freedom; in the classes, the students were entitled to ask questions and to discuss themes with the teacher – indeed, their reputation depended heavily on their success in such sessions of debate and discussion.[20]

THE EARLY DEVELOPMENT OF EDUCATION

Initially, the learning process of the Muslims started with the Prophet who himself used to teach his companions the principles of Islam. When he migrated to Medina, he immediately started the process of eradicating illiteracy. His mosque also served as a centre for Muslim learning. He was so interested in this matter that, soon after the victory of Badr, he instructed each of the Meccan captives, who were literate, to teach ten Muslims how to read and write as a condition for their release.[21] He also sent teachers and missionaries to different parts of Arabia so that they could teach the newly converted Muslims the principles of Islam.[22] He also set up circles of learned men to study and teach the Quran. Later, mosques were set up in every locality and since then have remained as the essential location for educational activities among the Muslims. The Prophet's example as a teacher constituted a sacred precedent for his followers. Hence they considered it their duty to set up mosques and schools in their domain. In the course of time, the simple pattern of the Prophet's school developed into a comprehensive and coherent educational system, fully integrated into the social and economic way of life.[23] This educational system was based on moral and spiritual qualities. It recognised no separation between sacred and secular. Indeed it 'breathed in a universe of sacred presence'. Whatever was known contained a profoundly religious feature, not only because the object of every type of knowledge is created by God, but also because the intelligence by which man knows is in itself a Divine gift. The education system therefore dealt with the whole being of the person whom it sought to educate. Its aim was not only the training of the mind but also the entire personality of the student. The teacher in this system was the transmitter of knowledge as well as the trainer of souls. Even the term 'teacher' in itself gained the meaning of trainer. It was embodied with ethical connotations which in the modern world have almost disappeared from the process of teaching and the transmission of knowledge, especially at the higher levels of education. The Islamic educational system neither separated the training of the mind from that of the soul, nor regarded the transmission of knowledge or its possession to be legitimate without the possession of proper moral and spiritual principles. Indeed, the acquisition of knowledge without these principles was regarded as very dangerous both to individuals and society.[24]

However, despite the fact that the Islamic educational system encompassed the whole life of traditional Muslims, certain distinct phases can be discerned. The first stage started at home where both parents acted as teachers in matters such as religion, language, culture and social customs. This period was followed by the Quranic schools (*al-Kuttab*) corresponding to elementary school. The aims of these schools were to enable the child to read and write the Quran, and to master the language as well as learn other subjects such as proverbs, poetry and, later, arithmetic. These schools formed the preparatory stage for higher studies where the students could then attend the *Madrasah*. The *Madrasah*[25] often incorporated the *Jamiah* which can be said to correspond at one and the same time, to secondary school as well as to college and university education.[26] The activities of these *Madrasahs* were divided into two parts. The religious or the transmitted sciences, and the intellectual sciences. The religious sciences included the study of the Quran, the *Hadith*, linguistics and theology and they dominated the educational activity of most *Madrasahs*. The intellectual sciences included the study of logic, mathematics, and the natural sciences, as well as philosophy. These divisions of the sciences were reflected in the curriculum of the *Madrasahs* and were taught alongside each other. These *Madrasahs* enjoyed a high position in society and, in the course of time, they developed into fully fledged educational institutions performing an important role throughout the Muslim world, such as the *Qayrawan* in Morocco and *al-Azhar* in Egypt. Later on, we find the development of a university system with several campuses such as *al-Nizamiyyah* and *al-Mustansiriyah* in Baghdad and *al-Nuriyyah* in Damascus.[27] In addition to the *Madrasahs* where theoretical learning was conducted, there were a number of observatories and hospitals. Some of them acted independently as institutions of scientific learning and experimentation, others were appended to the colleges. Al-Mamun's famous *Shamsiyyah* observatory was a most remarkable example. It was followed in many other cities. Moreover, these higher institutions continually provided society with its intellectual elite, and socio-political thinkers. Member of this elite functioned not only as teachers in the intellectual sense, but also as models of moral behaviour. Finally, Islam, by means of its educational system, successfully managed to preserve the ancient Greek and Eastern learning and then transmitted it to the Latin West. Hence its definition as the 'intermediate civilization'.[28]

EDUCATION OF WOMEN

Islam strongly encourages the education of women both in religious and social domains. Their education and cultural training were regarded as an integral dimension of social development.[29] There is no priority for men over women in relation to the right to education. Both are equally encouraged to acquire education, as already shown, 'from the cradle to the grave'.[30] Indeed all the Quranic verses which relate to education and which advocate the acquisition of knowledge were directed to both men and women alike. In accordance with the all-embracing concept of *Tawhid* – Oneness – when Islam elevated women physically by abolishing female infanticide, it could not overlook the need for their mental and spiritual elevation.[31] By contrast, Islam would view the neglect of these dimensions as virtually tantamount to murdering their personality. The Quran says: 'They are losers who besottedly have slain their children by keeping them in ignorance'.[32] Neither the Quran nor the sayings of the Prophet prohibit or prevent women from seeking knowledge and having an education. As already said, the Prophet was the forerunner in this regard, in declaring that seeking knowledge is obligatory upon every Muslim man and woman. By making such a statement, the Prophet opened all the avenues of knowledge for men and women alike. So, like her male counterpart, each woman is under a moral and religious obligation to seek knowledge, develop her intellect, broaden her outlook, cultivate her talents and then utilise her potential to the benefit of her soul and of her society. The interest of the Prophet in female education was manifest in the fact that he himself used to teach the women along with the men;[33] he also instructed his followers to educate not only their women but their slave girls as well.[34] The following *Hadith* puts it thus: a man who educates his slave girl, frees her and then marries her, this man will have a double reward.[35] The wives of the Prophet, especially Aisha, not only taught women, they taught men also and many of the Prophet's companions and followers learned the Quran, *Hadith* and Islamic jurisprudence from Aisha. Also, there was no limitation placed on women's education. Women were allowed to learn all the branches of science. She was free to choose any field of knowledge which interested her. Nonetheless, it is important to stress that, because Islam recognised that women are in principle wives and mothers, they should also place special emphasis on seeking knowledge in those branches which could help them in those particular spheres.[36]

In accordance with the dictates of the Quran and the *Hadith* encouraging women to develop all aspects of their personality, it was believed that an educated Muslim woman should not only radiate her moral qualities in the environment of her home, but she should also have an active role in the broad fields of social, economic and political development. The Quran, in particular (9:71–72), commands men and women to perform their prayers, pay their poor-tax and enjoin good and forbid evil in all forms: social, economic and political. This means that both have an equal duty to accomplish these tasks. In order to do so, they must have equal access to educational opportunities. For how can a woman uphold good social and economic policies or disapprove them if she is intellectually not equipped for the task?[37] Following the injunctions of the Quran and the Sunnah concerning female education, early Muslim women seized this opportunity and laboured to equip themselves in all branches of the knowledge of their time. They attended classes with men, they participated in all cultural activities side by side with them and managed to win their encouragement and respect.[38] Early Islamic history is replete with examples of Muslim women who showed a remarkable ability to compete with men and excelled them on many occasions. The following is a brief summary of the role played by Muslim women in different domains.

EARLY ACTIVITIES OF MUSLIM WOMEN

Religious Studies. This was the favourite subject for women in early Islam, and a considerable number of Muslim women managed to become notable figures among traditionists and jurists.[39] On top of the list was Aisha, the wife of the Prophet. She was a renowned scholar of her time. Her foresight and advice in the affairs of the Islamic community were regarded as highly important by the early Islamic rulers. She was credited with thousands of traditions received directly from the Prophet and is to the present day considered a great authority on Islamic Jurisprudence. Another famous name in this subject was Nafisah, a descendant of Ali who was a prominent jurist and theologian. It is mentioned that Al-Shafi'i, the founder of one of the schools of *Fiqh* used to attend her lessons and public lectures.[40] Shuhda as well was a renowned name in the subject of tradition, especially *Hadith*, which is a branch of Muslim science which was thought to be exclusively for men.[41]

Literature. Muslim women proved their ability to master this subject and achieved a high reputation among their contemporaries. In the forefront was al-Khansa, the greatest poetess of her day. Her poetry has survived into the present period. She was admired by the Prophet himself when he said that her poetry was unsurpassed.[42] In addition one could mention Qatilah who composed a famous elegy on the death of her brother which, again, was praised by the Prophet.[43]

Medicine. The humanitarian duties were performed by women in all the battles fought in Islam.[44] It was a custom that Muslim women accompanied the troops, so that they could bandage the wounded, fetch the water, transport the casualties back to Medina and instil courage in the men whose spirits were flagging.[45] It is said that when the Muslim troops were preparing to conquer Khaiber, Umayyah bint Qays-al-Ghaffariyyah, with a group of women, asked to be allowed to accompany the army. The Prophet granted them his permission and they performed their duties well. In addition, Muslim women attained a high status as medical scholars such as Zainab of the Bani Awd tribe who was a prominent physician and an expert oculist. Umm al-Hasan bint al-Qadi Abi Jafar al-Tanjali was a renowned woman of broad knowledge in different subjects, and was especially famous as a doctor.[46]

Military Service. Muslim women proved to be good warriors and they fought side by side with men. They achieved a considerable degree of success, and on occasion played very important military roles. In this respect mention should be made of Nusaiba, the wife of Zaid Ibn Asim, who took part in the famous battle of 'Ohud'. In that battle she fought vigorously and in the critical time when the Prophet was left alone she fought alongside him and wounded 11 persons with her sword. In the same battle, Nusaiba bint Kab al-Mazinia headed the Prophet's army against the enemy forces and at a crucial moment managed to mimimise the losses of the Muslim army. Of her the Prophet remarked 'Wherever I looked I saw her fighting before me'. Al-Yarmuk battle is another example in which Muslim women participated effectively. They were equal with men in the use of the sword. Hind bint Utbah was remarkable in this regard as was bint al-Harith Ibn Hisham.[47]

In addition, Muslim women also proved their ability to play a constructive role in other activities of the community. For example, they were involved in the political issues of the time and their opinions in political affairs were highly respected. They often took part in the process of choosing the Caliph.[48] They also enjoyed full freedom to express their ideas and were encouraged to participate in the social life of the community. Public life was like a stage where both men and women were actively involved. In the early period of Islam women used to discuss and debate with the Prophet[49] and his companions and even protect their rights if they were breached. It is said that during the time of the second Caliph Omar, a woman expressed her disagreement with him publicly in matters relating to the women's dowry and managed to correct him.[50] The Quran encourages women to speak their minds and not to be silent; nonetheless we see today some fundamentalists propagating the unfounded slogan that 'the voice of woman is *A'wrah* (private parts to be covered up)[51] and therefore arguing that it is in her best interest to keep quiet. For how can a woman learn and grow intellectually if she is not allowed to speak and communicate with others? How can she widen her understanding of things around her and speak forcefully and impressively if she is prevented from debating with others publicly?

ISLAM AND WORK OPPORTUNITIES FOR WOMEN

At a time when Muslim countries could benefit greatly from women's contribution to the development process, it becomes critically important to evaluate the position of Islam in relation to the employment of women. To start with, we can say that Islam does not forbid women to work and have a job outside the home so long as her external work does not interfere with her home obligations nor lower her dignity.[52] On the contrary, Islam granted woman the right to hold a job and to involve herself actively in trade and commerce. She is entitled to work outside her home and earn a living. During the early Islamic period women often helped men in their outdoor work and were allowed to move about freely among men.[53] Asma, the daughter of the first Caliph Abu-Bakr, used to help her husband in his field work.[54] The Prophet himself praised women who worked hard and well; he also encouraged women, including his wives and daughters, to engage themselves in gainful work. He used to say 'The most blessed earning is that which a person gains from his own labour'.[55] Women in early Islam even held formal posts of authority in the community such as al-Shafa' bint Abdullah who was appointed by the second Caliph Omar as superintendent of markets in Medina many times.[56] Hence, women can work as teachers, doctors, lawyers; they can work as employers or senior managers and they can work as Judges. It must be stressed that up until the present time and in most Muslim countries with the exception of Tunisia and Malaysia, the position of Judge is still regarded as a male domain. Therefore, women in these countries have traditionally been prevented from assuming this position. The ban has no legal foundation in either the scripture or the Sunnah. On the contrary, Aisha, the wife of the Prophet, was the forerunner in undertaking the position. She acted as a Judge during the era of the first three Caliphs. Also, Abu Hanifa, the founder of one of the schools of law states that a woman might become a Judge and consider all matters except the ones that are under the penal code. Jarir al-Tabari, the famous commentator on the Quran, gives women the right to be appointed as Judge without any conditions.[57] However, despite the fact that the external work of the woman was allowed and respected, a housewife, unable to work due to domestic responsibilities, did not feel that her contribution was less honourable and less fruitful.[58]

THE DECLINE IN STATUS OF MUSLIM WOMEN

The high status granted to women by the Quranic reforms which prevailed during the early Islamic period did not last long. Firstly, certain pre-Islamic customs reappeared, especially during the Abbasid period; secondly, various social attitudes infiltrated Islamic culture from conquered peoples, and were assimilated as norms and then identified with Islam. Hence the status of Muslim women started to deteriorate. This was accelerated by catastrophic historical events such as the Mongol and Turkish invasions and the ensuing decline of the Islamic civilisation. The ambience generated by these conditions served to undermine the position of Muslim women who became less and less part of social life in general.[59] They were neglected and treated as sex objects, assumed heavy veiling and were confined to their small circle of womenfolk with no contact outside their homes; they were prevented from participating in the public life of the community and excluded from public worship in the mosque. But the worst deprivation of all was the denial of their right to receive education.[60]

It was believed that basic awareness of the religious rites and memorising part of the Quran was sufficient for women. Therefore, while girls were welcome to all religious instruction especially in the lower grades, they were prevented from having further knowledge and education.[61] In fact the opposition to female education reached its peak when condemnation was voiced against teaching women the art of writing: 'He the teacher must not instruct any woman or female slave in the arts of writing, for thereby would accrue to them only an increase of deprav-ity'.[62] Thus their role in society centred mainly on preparing them to be good and obedient wives and mothers.[63] Later, when modern education became available, women were denied access to it and only schools for boys were initially developed. Female education was constrained by inherited social customs. Education for women came to be viewed as being of secondary importance to keeping the home and the family.[64] 'A woman's mission is to be a good wife and a compassionate mother ... an ignorant rural woman is better for the nation than one thousand female Lawyers or attorney generals'.[65] Female education was viewed as a threat to the traditional customs and the way of life of these societies. Indeed, educated women were feared and mistrusted as they could communicate potentially destructive or innovative ideas. Educated women were considered to be obtrusive and assertive. They did not appeal to men who expected them to serve them obediently. In addition, leaving home to go to school was in contrast with the idea of women segregation. The Islamic ideal of women's education and intellectual development was thus distorted, confused and actively opposed. The result was a disaster. The illiteracy of Muslim women reached a peak and became a widespread phenomenon in the world of Islam.[66]

Consequently, women throughout the Muslim world became ignorant not only of outside affairs, but also of their legal rights in terms of marriage, divorce and inheritance. Very often due to their ignorance of these rights, they were cheated, deceived and misled. This rendered Muslim women unable to claim and defend the rights guaranteed them by Islam.[67] This situation continued up to recent times, until efforts were made to improve female education in different parts of the Muslim world. However, despite these efforts and the rapid progress which has been achieved in the past four to five decades, the opportunities for women's education in the Muslim world, especially in the Middle East, still lag far behind those for men. Nothing substantial has been achieved, despite the fact that all Muslim countries have encouraged the spread of female education, stated that their aim is to try and raise the educational level of women, and proclaimed their intention to attain universal literacy. The accomplishment of these goals seems very far off. The gap between female and male literacy rates in several places is increasing and the overall level of illiteracy is extremely high.[68] The Islamic world, especially the Arab world, is amongst the areas in the world which has the highest rate of illiteracy amongst women, the lowest level of schooling for girls and the smallest number of women in paid employment. In 1991, the illiteracy rate among females in Afghanistan was 86 per cent, in Pakistan 78 per cent, in Egypt 66 per cent and in Iran 56 per cent. Although women's literacy varies enormously from country to country and also from area to area in any particular country, women in the Arab world are still a small minority among the student population. In every country the rate of male literacy is much higher than female literacy. Even in those countries which have initiated some reforms, there are still considerable disparities between male and female literacy,[69] as well as major discrepancies between the type of female education offered and the socio-economic needs of the various Arab countries.[70] This has been caused by many factors such as: family attitudes toward female education which still prevail, especially in the rural areas, where the majority of the Muslim population lives;[71] and the high female drop out rate due to the inequality between urban and rural education.[72] But the most important factor so far has been the historical interpretation of the jurists. This has taken the shape of a clear deviation from genuine Islamic principles by its strong opposition to female education. This factor is still very strong in Muslim society, particularly Arab society, and it influences government policy on education options and opportunities for women.[73] Saudi Arabia presents a clear example where Islam has been used to first deny and then discourage women's education.

SAUDI ARABIA AND FEMALE EDUCATION

In Saudi Arabia, a highly selective and narrow interpretation of Islam have had a restrictive impact upon the lives of women.[74] Traditionally, religion has been used as an excuse to justify the seclusion of women from the educational process. The rigid influence of the conservative theologians has played a critical role in suffocating female education for several decades through maintaining that girls should be prevented from all state primary and secondary schools.[75] Hence the low proportion of educated women in Saudi Arabia: in 1970, girls constituted about 30 per cent of elementary students, 20 per cent of secondary students and only 8 per cent of students in higher education.[76] In 1980, the literacy rate of male and female (15-year-olds) was 30 per cent to 2 per cent respectively. In 1985, the illiteracy rate among Saudi females was 57 per cent; in 1991 it was 51 per cent.[77]

The extremists argued that education of women would create immorality through corrupting their thinking and diverting their attention away from their essential role as good wives and mothers. They also voiced their fear that the outcome of the conflict of values brought about by such an educational transformation would result in discontent and instability both in the home as well as in society. It was under such pressure that public education for women in the Kingdom did not start until 1960.[78]

EDUCATION OF WOMEN IN SAUDI ARABIA SINCE 1960

Female education was introduced in Saudi Arabia in 1960, when the former King Faisal took the decision to set up schools for girls. Initially, the attempt met with strong opposition from the extremists who demonstrated their disagreement by gathering at the gates of the schools, expressing their displeasure with the new schools and with those who registered their daughters in them. National Guards had to be called to restore order. The opposition continued, unabated, until the government made two essential concessions: first, the government pledged that female education would be in line with Saudi customs, especially that of rigid segregation. Secondly, it set up a special body called the 'General Presidency for Girls' Education' to be responsible for girls' education. As a gesture of its commitment to preserve Saudi customs, the government placed this body under the control of the Saudi religious authorities who, since then, continue to supervise the education of girls in the Kingdom.[79]

THE DEVELOPMENT OF FEMALE EDUCATION IN SAUDI ARABIA

With this compromise, opposition to female education was finally mitigated and schools for girls were eventually established. The idea of schools for girls seems now to be accepted and the number of females enrolled in the educational process is increasing every year. However, despite the fact that female education in Saudi Arabia is becoming popular, and the statistics show that significant gains have been accomplished, equal opportunity between men and women is still far from being reached. This is even more the case in respect of female education in the rural areas, which is an elusive goal yet to be attained.[80] In fact the policy of female education in Saudi Arabia has been founded on limited bases, aimed more at discouraging than promoting the learning process; this process neither satisfies the needs of Saudi women nor corresponds to the socio-economic requirements of the country. In the elementary schools, for example, girls mostly learn those courses which are assumed to be suitable for them in their traditional role in Saudi society. These courses emphasise mainly the Arabic language, home economics, child caring and religious instruction.[81]

Although the elementary schools have been set up almost everywhere in the Kingdom, the proportion of female drop out after this primary level is still very high, and is a cause of great concern. As the level of education increases, the opportunity for girls to advance or progress become fewer. This is due to the fact that not all levels of knowledge and education available are at the location where the girls happen to be living, and also because in Saudi society women are not allowed to live alone in a residential campus. Hence it is difficult for them to move close to the educational institutions. Secondary schools, for instance, are not available everywhere in the country, neither are colleges. Vocational education too has been extremely limited except for nursing schools and tailoring centres. As regard university education, the situation is no better. The universities in Saudi Arabia are mainly for males, although some of them have branches in their departments for females. In these branches there is strict segregation of the sexes in classes and all teachers are female. Sometimes, due to the lack of suitable female teachers, the learning process is accomplished through the use of closed-circuit television. This enables male professors to lecture and answer female questions, without coming into contact with them.[82] Moreover, females in Saudi universities are not allowed to pursue any subject they like, being formally deprived of certain kinds of education. Up to 1974, the dominant areas were commerce, humanities and education. In 1975, women for the first time were allowed to enter the faculty of Medicine. This was followed by the admission to the faculty of Dentistry in 1980.[83] Other subjects such as Geology, Law, Engineering and Petroleum Studies are available in Saudi Arabia only for males; women are denied access to these fields. Three out of seven universities in the Kingdom do not accept women to these fields.[84] Women also find it difficult to have easy access to the university facilities such as the library. Hence the quality of girls' higher education is much lower than that for boys. Therefore, young Saudi women barely think of continuing their education beyond what is available, let alone considering education as a means of entering a career.[85]

CONCLUSION

In dealing with women's education from the Islamic perspective, it is recognised that wider issues pertaining to a modern Islamic curriculum have not been addressed. The latter is, indeed, a crucial issue, but our concern here has been one of the key questions of principle that should surely guide current attempts to formulate an authentically Islamic education system, namely the approach to women's education in such a system.

The case of Saudi Arabia was selected not to attack this particular system; there are a number of Muslim countries which could have been criticised on this central issue. The reason for focusing briefly on Saudi Arabia is that this country is regarded as 'traditional' and ostensibly closer to Islamic cultural norms than the other Muslim countries. Therefore, I have felt it important to highlight the great discrepancy between, on the one hand, the genuine Islamic position vis-à-vis women's education, and, on the other, the policy expressed in Saudi Arabia.

To briefly recapitulate: we have found that women in the early Islamic period were not only socially active, but were encouraged in all the main branches of learning and indeed rose to positions of great eminence. In stark contrast to this, we have seen that in Saudi Arabia the picture is one of seclusion from society and exclusion from certain areas of learning and hence employment opportunities. These attitudes to women can be attributed much more directly to inherited socio-cultural norms – assimilated from non-Islamic cultures or re-emerging out of pre-Islamic practices, as has been argued here – rather than to any Islamic principles on this question.

The position of Islam on women's education, as on so many other issues, aims at a balance, a 'middle way' – (as Islam is so often called). That is, recognising that women are in principle wives and mothers whilst not allowing this recognition to block avenues of self-development for women as individuals in their own right; and conversely, the dignity and value of being a wife and a mother should not be diminished by the concept of equality of educational opportunity. In Islam, the choice is not an 'either-or' one; there is no necessary contradiction between affirming the sacred role of women in the home *and* respecting the right of women to participate in social activities outside the home. So long as the education system is governed by the spirit of Islam throughout, there will be a harmony between these two modes of social activity, permitting women to express themselves in accordance with their natural dispositions, and to be given the respect and honour which is so central to the real social message of Islam.

3 Women and Marriage in Islam

Marriage is without doubt one of the most important institutions of human society. As such, God has set rules and regulations to ensure that the attainment of marriage is possible for everyone. The Quran indicates that the real and natural way to gain peace and satisfaction in life is through a husband–wife relationship, just as Adam and Eve did beforehand; it is only through this arrangement that peace in married life can really be achieved and guaranteed. In human society, therefore, the main principle of matrimonial life is that the human race should live in pairs,[1] that is: a man and a woman should marry each other and live together in happy union.[2]

Islam assigns great importance to marriage. Indeed, it is highly recommended on religious, moral and social grounds.[3] Marriage in Islam is regarded as a strong bond and a total commitment to life, to society and to being a respectable human. It is a promise that the married couple make to one another and to God. This undertaking on the part of the married partners would allow them to find mutual fulfilment and self-realisation, love and peace, comfort and hope. This is because marriage in Islam is essentially a righteous act and an act of complete devotion. As such, celibacy is discouraged not only for men, but for women as well.[4] This is in consideration of the fact that their needs are equally legitimate and valid. Indeed, Islam views marriage as a natural course for women in the same way as it is for men, and probably even more so in view of the fact that marriage guarantees women some form of economic security. It must be stressed here that this benefit for women is in no way an indication that marriage in Islam is sheer economic transaction. Indeed, the economic factor is the least aspect of the whole enterprise; the emphasis has been always on the religious qualities[5] of the spouses.[6]

THE SIGNIFICANCE OF MARRIAGE IN ISLAM

Islam views marriage to be of benefit to both the individual as well as to society.[7] As such, the gains resulting from it outweigh any shortcomings.[8] From the collective point of view the most significant benefit is of course procreation, but not just the physical perpetuation of the human race;

rather, the institution of marriage ensures that this procreative function will be both sanctified and orderly, not vulgar and chaotic. From the specifically religious point of view, having children entails the following: the realisation of God's desire;[9] the fulfilment of the Prophet's call to marry and increase his followers' number; gaining the fruit of a child's prayer. Muslims believe that when parents die and leave a child (son or daughter – the gender issue in this context does not make any difference), his prayer would benefit the dead parents.[10] However, if the child dies before his parents, he would make intercession on his parents' behalf.[11]

Fulfilling one's sexual desire is another important aspect of marriage. Marriage, from the Islamic viewpoint, helps control sexual passion and channel it in the right direction. Also, it functions as a shield against committing adultery and fornication, both of which are forbidden in Islam.[12] Marriage, moreover, brings peace and tranquillity of spirit and implants love and compassion between the married partners. These are great supports for one's worship of God. Intimacy between spouses is viewed as catalyst for the development of their souls. In other words, the intimate relationship that develops between a husband and wife is crucial for relieving the heart from its burdens and thus enables the mind to better focus on accomplishing the Divine requirements. Al-Ghazali beautifully explains this point in the following account: 'The third benefit of marriage is that the heart finds ease through intimacy with women, because of sitting and joking with them. This ease then becomes the cause of an increase in desire for worship. For diligence in worship brings weariness, and the heart contracts. But ease acquired in this way brings back the heart's strength. Ali said, 'Do not remove rest and ease completely from the hearts, lest they become blind'. It sometimes happened that the Prophet was overcome by such tremendous unveilings that his bodily frame was not able to tolerate it. He would take Aisha's hand and say, 'Talk with me, Aisha'. He wanted to gain strength so that he could carry the burden of revelation. Once he came back to this world and gained full strength, the thirst for that work would overcome him, and he would say, 'Give us ease, Bilal'. Then he would turn back to the ritual prayer. Sometimes the Prophet would strengthen his mind with a sweet aroma. That is why he said, 'Three things of this world of yours were made lovable to me: women, perfume and the coolness of my eye [as] was placed in the ritual prayer'. He put ritual prayer last because that is the goal. For he said, 'The coolness of my eye is in the ritual prayer', while sweet aromas and women are the ease of the body. Thereby the body gains strength to busy itself with prayer and to gain the coolness of the eye found therein'.[13]

Islam also sees marriage as an instrument which creates a comfortable home for both spouses. The marital link helps the partners to work together and co-operate amicably in the management of the domestic affairs of their house; hence sufficient time could be spared to meet the Divine commandments. Therefore, the Prophet is reported to have advised his followers to choose the right spouses who would help them attain Divine blessings. He said[14] 'Seek to have a grateful heart, a sweet tongue and a believing, righteous wife who would help you in your endeavour to succeed on the Last Day'.[15]

Marriage, in addition, is seen as an opportunity to develop for oneself a good and sound character as a result of the added family responsibility which both spouses have to endure during their married life. Hence, success in carrying out family commitments (which are equally regarded as divine duties) would ensure Divine reward. The Prophet said 'A man will be rewarded for what he spends on his wife, even for putting a morsel of food into her mouth'. Also, 'Whoever performs his prayers correctly, and spends on his children in spite of his modest means, and does not speak ill against others, will be in paradise as close to me as these [two fingers of mine]'.[16] Finally, marriage ensures social stability and a dignified form of living for both partners (the husband and the wife), probably even more for women since it guarantees their rights both as wives as well as mothers (of course alongside their rights as individuals).[17]

CONDITIONS OF MARRIAGE

Since Islam takes marriage seriously, its concern has been always to ensure that the marriage bond stays relatively stable and durable. To achieve these goals, it has laid down certain rules and regulations to meet these objectives. First, the couple have to be of proper marriageable age;[18] also, there should be no discrepancy between their ages. It must be stressed that the claim by some scholars that the groom has to be always senior in age so as to ensure a healthy marriage relationship has no religious grounds and in practical terms does not make any sense. In fact, it contradicts the practice of the Prophet, two of whose wives (Khadija and Sauda) happened to be older than him; despite this, the record shows that they lived in peace and harmony. Second, there should be a degree of compatibility between the two partners in terms of social status, educational standards and physical attraction (again the claim by some scholars that the bride has to be more beautiful and more attractive than her groom is a fallacy). Third, the dowry of the bride should be of a reasonable level: neither too high, which could cause hardship for both of them, nor too low which might give the impression that the bride is of no worth. The dowry – which is in its essence a gift from the groom to the bride – should be affordable and manageable so as to ensure satisfaction and happiness on both sides. Fourth, the consent of the couple is crucial for the stability and durability of the marriage. Both have to enter into the wedlock with free will and without coercion. Compelling the couple (or even just one of them) to contract an unsatisfactory union would be detrimental to the interest of both sides and could lead to a disastrous end. Fifth, the prospective partners have to be pious and of good moral conduct.[19] Both have to be kind, sympathetic, considerate, patient and loving, caring to one another; this encourages peace and harmony in domestic life. Sixth, the two parties have to declare, from the beginning, their intentions to keep the marital bond as permanent as humanly possible. This commitment requires that the marriage contract should be free of any hidden agenda such as casual or temporary unions. Therefore, Islam is against all marriages that have been described as experimental, casual and temporary.[20] In a clear statement, the Prophet outrightly denounced those men and women who enjoy the frequent change of marital partners and warned against their unacceptable behaviour. Having stated the importance Islam lays on the permanency of marriage, it is essential to stress that in Islam there is no concept of 'indissoluble' marriage. Although Islam endeavours to keep the marital link stable and intact, this does not mean that the wedlock cannot be brought to an end if there are compelling circumstances. Indeed, Islam recognises that if the marriage is not working, it is in the interest of both sides to terminate it on good terms. Hence, divorce in Islam is a legitimate act, although it is discouraged by the Prophet.[21]

Islam, as we know, encourages both men and women to marry. Just like a man, a Muslim woman (virgin or non-virgin) has the freedom to propose to a man of her liking, either orally or in writing (I wonder how many Muslim women these days would dare to initiate an oral proposal, let alone put it in writing!). Listen to the following: 'Umamah bint Abil-As was one lady companion of the Prophet who proposed for marriage in writing. She sent a message to al-Mugheerah bin Maufal saying: "If you feel you stand in need of us then proceed forth". He then sought her hand in marriage from al-Hassan, her cousin, who duly solemnised the marriage'. Also, a Muslim lady made an oral proposal to the Prophet himself in the following account: 'I present myself to you'. She then waited for quite some time while the Prophet kept looking at her. A man said to the Prophet: 'If you do not need her, please marry me to her'. The Prophet asked him, 'Do you have anything to offer as dowry?' (The man did not have anything to offer except his loin cloth, which after all he could not afford to give away. However, after lengthy enquiries, he offered to teach her the Quran). The Prophet then declared: 'I solemnise your marriage with her with whatever verses of the Quran you have as dowry'.[22]

The Muslim woman, therefore, has the freedom of marital choice: she is at liberty to choose her prospective husband, look at him and get to know him[23] without coercion on the part of the father or other relatives. If force or pressure takes place, she has the right to appeal to the court to redress the wrong.[24] Her consent is essential for the validity of the marriage contract. The Prophet is reported to have made the following statements: 'A previously married woman shall not be married till she gives her consent, nor should a virgin be married till her consent is sought'. 'A previously married woman is more a guardian for herself than her guardian, and a virgin should be asked permission about herself, and her permission is her silence'. 'A grown-up girl shall be asked permission about herself. If she is silent, it is her permission; and if she declines, there shall be no compulsion on her'.[25]

According to Islam, a divorced or widowed woman has the right to re-marry without any shame or denunciation. In fact, the Quran allows the betrothal of a divorced or widowed woman even during her period of transition (*idda*). 'It shall be no offence for you openly to propose marriage indirectly to such women or to cherish them in your hearts. Allah knows that you will remember them. Do not arrange to meet them in secret and, if you do, speak to them honourably. But you shall not consummate the marriage before the end of their waiting period. Know that Allah has knowledge of all your thoughts. Therefore take heed and bear in mind that Allah is forgiving and merciful'.[26] Also, neither age nor previous marriage would impede a woman from contracting perfect matches. Many are the examples which can be cited from the early Muslim community during which women were, very often, re-married after they were divorced or widowed, and this was done without stigma or discredit.

Take, for instance, Umm-Kulthum bint Aqba, an early convert from Mecca. She emigrated to Medina in defiance of her family, who tried to force her to return to Mecca, but to no avail. She stayed in Medina and married her first husband, Zaid bin Harith. When Zaid was killed in one of the battles she contracted a second marriage with Zubayr bin al-Awwam. Zubayr was rough with her, so she decided to part with him. After the separation, she married Abdel Rahman bin Awf, her third husband, and bore him two sons. Upon Abdel Rahman's death, Umm Kulthum once more contracted herself into marriage, to her fourth and final husband, this time with the conqueror of Egypt, Amr ibn al-As. She stayed with him until she passed away.[27]

Atika bint Zaid is another good example. She was a woman of exceptional abilities who had managed to contract four marriages during her lifetime. Her first husband was Abdullah ibn Abu Bakr, son of the first Caliph Abu Bakr. He died, leaving her a fortune on condition that she would not re-marry. For a while she was content with the idea of living a celibate life, but later she decided to go against his wish and not to spend the rest of her life alone; hence her decision to accept Umar ibn al-Khattab, the second Caliph, as her second husband. When Umar was assassinated in 642 she married her third husband, Zubayr ibn al-Awwam. After his death in 656, she took her fourth husband, Hussein ibn Ali, son of the fourth Caliph Ali; by this time she was around forty-five years old.[28]

Contract and Conditions

Marriage in Islam requires a contract between two equal partners. Hence, in Islamic terms, the woman is to be a subject rather than an object in the marriage contract. The contract, in sum, is a legal written document between two adults, which entails an offer by one partner and an acceptance by the other in the presence of two witnesses. The Qadi, or official, usually solemnises the marriage in a mosque or court or any other location. The consent of the prospective wife is crucial for the effectiveness of the marriage contract. Any force or blackmail on the part of the relatives would automatically render the contract invalid.[29] The bride, moreover, has the exclusive right to stipulate her own conditions in the contract. These conditions include mainly (though not exclusively) such issues as marriage terms (the right, for example, to have a monogamous relationship whilst she is still living with her husband) and divorce terms (the right, for instance, to dissolve the marital bond at her own initiative if she deems it necessary).[30] In addition, dowries – one initial and another deferred in case of divorce – must be specified and written down and they should be of substance. The dowry (or *Mahr*, in Islamic terms) belongs to the wife; it is her exclusive right and it should not be given away, neither to her family nor to her relatives.[31] The Quran says 'Give women their dowry as a free gift; but if they choose to make over to you a part of it, you may regard it as lawfully yours'.[32]

When the marriage is consummated, the couple assume a new relationship: that is, a husband–wife relationship. It is a kind of reciprocal and interdependent relationship. The Quran says 'And of His signs is that He gave you wives from among yourselves, that you might live in tranquillity with them, and put love and kindness in your hearts. Surely there are signs in this for thinking people'.[33] The verse implies that in a marriage bond the two partners are a comfort to each other. They should find and enjoy peace and tranquillity in each other's company and be bound together not only by a sexual relationship but also by love, compassion and mercy. As such, both have to demonstrate mutual care, affection, respect and be prepared to make sacrifices. Also, there should be no servility on the part of either side, for they are two equal partners in a healthy, loving and caring relationship.[34]

The Quran eloquently illustrates this equal partnership in the following statement: 'They are an apparel to you, as you are an apparel to them'.[35] The verse explains that just as a garment covers a person completely and provides him/her with warmth, protection and decency, in the same way a husband and wife provide each other with the necessary warmth, comfort, intimacy and protection.[36] The realisation of these principles in actual life depends, mainly, on the way both partners react to each other. In this context, the Quran expects them to behave in the best manner toward each other. The husband, on the one hand, is commanded to treat his wife gently and with kindness, affection and consideration. The Prophet said 'The best of you is the best of you to his wife, and I am better than any of you toward my wife'.[37] He is to deal with her with dignity and in an equitable manner, not to hurt or injure her feelings. He is to show her that he loves her,[38] appreciates her good qualities and he is to give her the impression that he needs her and depends on her to attain happiness in life. Also, he is asked to ensure that his tasks as husband and father are fulfilled to the utmost. Besides, the husband has to meet his legal responsibility to provide full maintenance of the wife: a task which he has to accomplish with good cheer and gladness. The wife, on the other hand, is similarly required to reciprocate in kindness towards her husband, treat him with respect, admire his good qualities and express her love and affection to him. Also, she is called upon to ensure that her duties as wife and mother are performed to the best of her abilities.[39]

To maintain a happy conjugal relationship, both partners must be loyal, honest, direct, and trustworthy. They should be thoughtful, sympathetic and sensitive towards each other's feelings; in particular, they must avoid raising each other's suspicions and jealousy and try to maintain their integrity as husband and wife, united together in a matrimonial link. Concerning their sexual intimacy, both must be pleasing[40] and receptive. They should endeavour to attain and give maximum gratification. Moreover, in order to keep the marital link intact, stable and healthy, both partners have to demonstrate their willingness to share the burden of looking after the welfare of the family. They must share the ups and downs of married life, be prepared to make sacrifices, pay attention to each other's point of view, consult each other and adopt joint decisions on important matters that affect the entire family.

These joint decisions have to be delivered or enforced by the husband since, in Islam, he is the head of the family. This is based on the following Quranic verses which give the husband the right to be in charge of the family: 'Women shall with justice have rights similar to those exercised against them, although men have a degree above women. Allah is Mighty and Wise'.[41] 'Men have authority over women because Allah has made the one superior to the other, and because they spend their wealth to maintain them'.[42] These verses were and still are a source of much discussion and debate throughout the Muslim world, generating a host of different interpretations. These interpretations range from liberal to moderate to conservative. Our view in this context is that the headship of the husband should on no account be a license for dictatorship; it should entail no absolute freedom on the part of the person in charge; if the husband mis-uses or abuses his status, the wife has the right to interfere to rectify the situation. After all, the whole issue of being a chair-person is to ensure the smooth running of the family. Any neglect on the part of the husband to fulfill the task which is designated to him justifies his replacement by the more able person (the wife).

However, God-conscious pairs would always act responsibly because they are aware of their commitments to God as well as to each other. Also, because they are conscious of the fact that if they live up to their promises and act rationally in their married life they would invoke God's pleasure, hence making their lives a perpetual joy and paradise. But, sadly, this kind of paradise, envisaged by the Quran and practised briefly during the Prophet's time, has hardly ever been realised. In fact, the case has nearly always been the reverse. Slowly but surely, attitudes towards women and marriage changed. The Quranic principles which bestowed honour, dignity, kindness and respect on women were gradually eroded and went into limbo. Customs, rather than Divine laws, shaped and continue to shape the social fabric of society and govern people's attitudes towards women and marriage. The outcome has been a steady deterioration in the status of women as far as their marital rights are concerned. Take, for example, the right to initiate a marriage proposal. This has been completely abandoned: not even in her wildest dreams would a woman dare to propose orally or in writing. The disappearance of this early practice has been so total that most women, even educated ones, are not aware of its existence, let alone practise it. The right to exercise her choice in selecting a marriage partner has, in most cases, been forgotten. Most marriages that currently take place in Muslim societies are arranged unions, during which force and intimidation are quite often employed to obtain the girl's consent. Moreover, her freedom to sign the marriage contract has been considerably curtailed. The majority of Muslim marriages nowadays are contracted through agents (guardians, especially on the part of the woman), very often a male member of the family (father, brother, or uncle), who formalises and signs the contract on her behalf. In doing so, her opportunity and right to negotiate marriage and divorce terms are deliberately denied. In most cases, a woman is subjected to considerable pressure to avoid stipulating in her marriage contract a divorce right or any other rights which might be viewed as a constraint on the freedom of the husband. If she did so, the social pressure on her would be so tremendous that in the end she would be obliged to give up, otherwise she would be accused of endangering the whole enterprise. Divorce has become a stigma and women are always regarded as being culpable. The prospects for a non-virgin (divorcee or widow) getting re-married is dim. Indeed, in many cases they are forced to spend the rest of their lives cherishing the memories of their dead husbands and serving the male members of their own families.

Within the context of a husband–wife relationship, authoritarianism and dictatorship have replaced the ideal and equal partnership advocated by the Quran. The husband assumes the role of ruler, superior, controller, oppressor and master, while the wife, on the other hand, is reduced to a slave, a captive, a low, inferior and submissive creature. Listen to what the so-called Council of Ulama (that is, people with knowledge about Islam) of South Africa has to say about the relationship between the two spouses: 'She (the wife) should mould herself to wholeheartedly submit to his whims and fancies. His likes must become her likes and his dislikes, her dislikes. She should step out of her way to comfort him and to console him in his worries and distress. Her wishes and desires are subservient to his wishes and orders .... After all (God) has created her for her husband's comfort and peace'. The Council goes on to say 'The Shariah has accorded the husband the highest degree of authority over his wife. Likewise it will transpire that the wife has to offer the higher degree of submission to her husband ... with humility and patience she should tolerate his shortcomings and even his injustice ... men are the rulers of women and they have a superior rank ... (as such) it is the husband's right and role to dominate and dictate (and) it is the duty of the wife to submit and serve. The wife should understand that she can never conquer her husband by confrontation and seeking to set herself up as his equal or superior'.[43] Concerning the financial arrangements between them, the Council stresses: 'It is significant that in spite of the wife remaining the sole owner of her wealth ... (she is encouraged) to put her wealth at his disposal and pleasure'. What about his money? 'She should not attempt to appoint herself as the controller of his finances. It is none of her business on whom her husband spends his wealth'. What if the husband fails to perform his duties properly? The Council emphasises: 'She must not adopt a legal stand and a technical attitude, demanding from her husband perfect and total fulfilment of her legal rights .... The wife has to remember that despite her husband's failure to fulfil his duties to her, she is under ... obligation to obey her husband ..., obedience to the husband will ensure the everlasting happiness ... for her'.[44]

The mutual responsibilities on both sides to demonstrate to each other their loyalty, honesty and respect have become exclusively the wife's domain and obligations. The husband has been deliberately left out of the equation. So whether he is honest and loyal or a cheat it does not matter. What matters most (and this is important to him and to the male-dominated society) is the faithfulness and loyalty of the wife. There is no question of reciprocity between them in this matter. I have not read a single book (obviously those written by men) which considers faithfulness obligatory upon both sides. The emphasis has always been on the wife, as if she is a creature with no control over her sexuality. The reader might consider it disgraceful to have such a mentality at the end of the twentieth century, but sadly we still do. Listen again to what the Council has to say: 'The outstanding virtue of a true Muslim wife is her total faithfulness to her husband. Her mind, her heart, her gaze and her body are only for her husband .... It does not behove the Muslim wife to cast her eyes on any man other than her husband ... even a glance at another man is considered infidelity and an act of unfaithfulness ... entertaining thoughts of other men in the mind is infidelity in Islam; glancing at other men is infidelity, speaking to other men is infidelity. Infidelity and unfaithfulness to the husband are not confined to adultery'. In other words, she has to bury herself alive. But what if the husband happens to be unfaithful? Well, 'The woman of intelligence and understanding should face this delicate situation with great patience ... she should endeavour to win over his heart with love and tender tones ... if the husband rebuffs her, she should not give up hope. Leave the matter for a while and resume (the advice) respectfully, humbly and intelligently at another time when he is in a better mood'. What if he marries a second wife? '(She) should not behave as if her world and life has ended ... she should face the situation with ... maturity and patience. She should suppress her urges and never vent her emotional feelings ... by behaving despicably, she will only harden her husband's feelings and to him she will start to appear like a witch ... (she) must accept her husband's second marriage and behave with respect and dignity .... A wife should learn a very important rule, viz. that a husband cannot be tamed and won over by nagging and quarrelling. To achieve success for her marriage the wife must be submissive and humble'.[45]

This is the kind of Islam which we usually hear, read about and most importantly see in actual life; it is a male-defined Islam. As such it is grossly against women. Equally important, it runs contrary to the very essence of the Divine message: that is to establish a happy conjugal relationship based on the principles of equality, impartiality, fairness and justice.

4 Women and the Question of Polygamy in Islam*

INTRODUCTION

In general, Western studies on Muslim women in Muslim societies have shown a tendency to assume that non-Western cultures ought to function according to Western norms. They tend to highlight certain practices in Muslim societies, examining them according to their own Western values. Hence it is often claimed not only that Muslim women are oppressed, suppressed, ill-treated, and subordinated, but also that these fundamental abuses of women's rights are natural concomitants of basic principles of the Islamic religion. In other words, Western studies on Muslim women, constricted within their own paradigm, tend to confuse Islam at the practical level with Islam at the ideal level. Very often, then, images of Muslim women in the world are constructed without studying Islam itself. The majority of Western studies attempt to explain the status of Muslim women through using statistical analysis and comparing the results with their own cultural areas, pointing out that Muslim countries have low rates of economic activity by women, low female literacy and low female school enrolment at all levels. Such data are used to justify specific hypotheses which they propose in regard to Muslim societies.[1] The use of statistical data on fertility rates is another example, deployed to show that Islam, by its nature, contains 'procreationalism' which leads to the confinement of Muslim women to child-rearing and discourages them from participating in outside social activities. Specific restrictive social practices, such as veiling and the seclusion of women, are referred to in vague terms such as 'Islamic restrictions' or 'Islamic tradition' without providing clear definitions.

Such studies, moreover, presume to demonstrate the inferior status of women in Muslim societies by pointing out the low employment rates among women in commercial and industrial activities. This type of analysis has little concrete grounds; indeed, only in some specific situations in industrial societies do the employment rates of women in commercial activities

---

* Some of the material in this Chapter has been previously published in the article 'The question of polygamy in Islam', *Muslim Education Quarterly*, The Islamic Academy, Cambridge, 1991, reproduced by kind permission of the publisher.

reflect women's position in society. Some closer consideration, taking into account the concept of economy in Islam and how it relates to women, would show that there is rarely a causal relationship between women's social status in society and their commercial and industrial activities.[2]

Another approach found among commentators focuses on the legal institutions concerning Muslim women, such as marriage, divorce, and inheritance; all of which look inequitable in their eyes. They stress that the legal instructions mentioned in the Quran and *Hadith* discriminate against women. They refer, for example, to the female portion of inheritance, which is half that of the male, as clear evidence of discrimination against women in Muslim societies. This approach ignores the historical and social background which frames these legal institutions, and it shows a lack of understanding of Islamic Jurisprudence – a prerequisite for any serious study of legal institutions in the Muslim world. From some Western perspectives, then, Muslim women are portrayed as oppressed, secluded and deprived of human rights. This image in large measure results from the lack of self-criticism and the ethnocentric approach to the study of Muslim women as described above. It is essential, then, to re-examine these Western images. In doing so, prejudices and biases could perhaps be clarified and avoided.[3] In Muslim World, Islam underlines much of the economic, political and ethical value system of the region. Islam is not a subsidiary element in society, but a fundamental one. Hence, in order to understand the position of women in the Muslim World, it is essential to understand the Islamic view concerning their position in Islamic law.[4] At the same time, such a study would not only further an understanding of this 'Islamic position', but, especially importantly, will allow more justified conclusions and insights to be reached about the very real disadvantages from which women in Muslim societies have suffered. Obviously, much of this is beyond the scope of the present study; my main concern in this chapter is to deal with one aspect of women's issues in the Muslim world: the question of polygamy.

The practice of polygamy in Islam continues to be one of the most controversial subjects concerning women and Islam. Misconceptions about this traditional Islamic institution are widespread and it is vigorously condemned by non-Muslims. Very often, when the question of Islam and marriage is approached, the first image conjured up in the mind of non-Muslims, is that Islam is a religion which encourages the sexual indulgence of the male members of the society and the subjugation of its females through this patrimonial system. Moreover, it is claimed that Islam has introduced and encouraged the practice of polygamy – which is therefore portrayed as confined to Muslims only.[5] The intention of this study is to show the falsity of such notions, on the one hand, whilst underlining the rigorous conditions which must be observed if the practice of polygamy is to be legitimate in strictly Islamic terms, on the other.

POLYGAMY:[6] AN OVERVIEW

From time immemorial (before Islam) polygamy was a well-known practice among most ancient nations. It was permitted and practised in Egypt, Persia and China. Also, it was practised by the Jews and was dictated in certain cases by the Mosaic law.[7] According to the teaching of the Talmud: 'A man may marry many wives, for Rabba saith it is lawful to do so, if he can provide for them. Nevertheless, the wise men have given good advice, that a man should not marry more than four wives'.[8]

The great prophets and religious leaders of the Old Testament were clearly polygamous. Abraham had more than one wife. He first married Sara who later gave birth to Isaac, the progenitor of the Israelites. Then he married Haggar who also bore him a son, Ishmael, the progenitor of the Arabs. David had one hundred wives and King Solomon is said to have contracted 700 marriages.[9] The practice of polygamy in Judaism continued until the eleventh century when it was prohibited during the convening of the Rabbinical Synod at Worms: 'Among European Jews polygany (see n6) was still practiced during the Middle Ages, and among Jews living in Muhammadan countries it occurs even to this day. An express prohibition of it was not pronounced until the convening of the Rabbinical Synod at Worms, in the beginning of the eleventh century. This prohibition was originally made for the Jews living in Germany and Northern France, but it was successively adopted in all European countries. Nevertheless, the Jewish marriage Code retained many provisions which originated at a time when polygany was still legally in existence'.[10]

In Christianity, although the New Testament endorses monogamy as an ideal form of marriage, it does not explicitly prohibit polygamy except in the case of a bishop and a deacon. The first Christian teachers did not find it necessary to condemn polygamy because monogamy was customary among peoples in whose midst Christianity was preached. Indeed, no church council in the earliest centuries condemned it, nor was any obstacle placed in the way of its practice.[11] On the contrary, many religious figures spoke of it with considerable tolerance. For example, Saint Augustine did not categorically condemn it nor did Luther, who approved the bigamous marriages of Philip of Hesse. Up to the sixteenth century, some German reformers accepted the validity of a second, even a third contractual marriage. In 1650, some Christian figures decided that every man must be allowed to marry two women. More recently, we find the doctrine of Brigham Young's Mormon sect, which endorsed the practice of polygamy until the late 1880s, when the United States Congress passed a resolution prohibiting the practice.[12] Polygamy was also customary among the tribes of Africa and Australia. Indeed the Hindu law of marriage does not restrict the number of wives a man is allowed to marry.[13]

On the whole, it is said that Christians are less polygamous than either Jews or Muslims. However, it is important to stress that Christianity did not introduce monogamy to the Western world, nor was it reinforced out of a need for social reform. Rather, monogamy was the only legal form of marriage in the Western society to which Christianity was first introduced. This was further strengthened by the fact that a strong tradition of formal monogamy was prevalent in Greece and Rome. Also, the fact that Christianity took root among the least wealthy free classes, who could not afford polygamy, further reinforced monogamy.[14]

ISLAM AND POLYGAMY

In pre-Islamic Arabia polygamy was a common practice; a man was allowed to marry an unlimited number of wives without any restrictions. The unlimited number of wives was justified as compensation for the shortage of men caused by the frequent tribal wars.[15] With the advent of Islam, the concept of polygamy was radically redefined. Islam limited the number of wives to four[16] (under certain conditions) and introduced monogamy as an ideal form of marriage.[17] Moreover, some forms of polygamy which were prevalent in Arabia were prohibited by Islam – such as marrying two sisters at the same time or a woman and her aunt, etc.[18]

The verse which permits polygamy was revealed to the Prophet after the battle of Ohud in which many Muslim men were killed. This raised concern for those women and orphans who were left behind without men to take care of them.[19] The verse reads as follows: 'If you fear that you cannot treat orphans with fairness, then you may marry such women as seem good to you: two, three, or four of them. But if you fear that you cannot do justice, marry one only or those you possess. This will make it easier for you to avoid injustice'.[20] This verse is often interpreted in conjunction with another verse in the same chapter. It says: 'In no way you can treat your wives in a just manner, even though you may wish to do that. Do not set yourself altogether against any of them, leaving her, as it were, in suspense. If you do what is right and guard yourselves against evil, (you will find) Allah Forgiving, Merciful'.[21]

Concerning the interpretation of these two verses, currently there are at least two main positions:[22] *the first position* prevails among some contemporary Muslim scholars who interpret the first verse (4: 3) as implying that polygamy is allowed only if there is no worry about the issue of injustice towards the wives, and it is forbidden if the husband doubts his ability to deal with them justly. Now, the argument continues, since treating one's wives justly is a *sine qua non* for the practice of polygamy, and since the second verse (4: 129) makes it crystal clear that a man will not be able to attain justice no matter how hard he tries, polygamy in the end is unlawful or forbidden. It must be stressed that one of the early advocates of this stance was the Egyptian scholar Muhammad Abduh who wrote extensively on the issue of polygamy and its implications for Muslim societies. Abduh believes that although taking more than one wife is permitted in Islam, this permission is conditioned by the fact that the husband should deal with them justly. Failing to do so he is to be satisfied with one wife only. He says: 'The Muhammadan law allows man to take up to four wives at a time if he thinks he is capable of treating them justly. But if he feels he is unable to fulfil this condition then he is forbidden to have more than one wife'.[23]

The question of dealing with one's wives justly means, from Abduh's viewpoint, the ability to achieve absolute justice, which is a prerequisite to practise polygamy. Since, in his opinion, this condition (absolute justice) is very difficult to obtain, the ban on polygamy becomes imperative to prevent any injustice towards the wives. Abduh also argues that since polygamy was initially introduced to meet special social, political, economic and military conditions within the Muslim community,[24] the change in those circumstances means that the practice of polygamy is no longer a necessity or a requirement. Muslim leaders, therefore, ought to restrict or ban the practice because of the change in the circumstances which led to its sanction in the first place. Moreover, he maintains that when polygamy was first sanctioned, the aim was to strengthen and consolidate the nascent Muslim community. This was accomplished, but with the passage of time the practice ceased to fulfil its role properly because it has been abused by uncommitted people, hence making it more harmful than beneficial. In view of this, Abduh asserts that it is in the interest of the community to withhold or ban the practice.[25]

Abduh's position on polygamy has influenced certain Muslim scholars and reformers in some Muslim countries, whose legislators have decided to incorporate his interpretation of the Quranic verses on polygamy within their system of law. For example, Tunisia has outlawed polygamy outright[26] and justified it by stressing that its action is in conformity with the

Quranic injunctions on the subject: the Quran says that a man is allowed to have up to four wives if he is able to treat them with absolute equality. However, since it is virtually impossible for a human being to achieve this condition, the ban on the practice is in accordance with the Divine Law. Other countries, such as Egypt, Iraq, Syria and Pakistan have all restricted the practice. The law in Egypt, for instance, insists that a man cannot contract a second marriage unless he obtains his first wife's permission beforehand. Syria and Iraq require authorisation from the Judge, while Pakistan demands written authorisation from the so-called Arbitration Council.

The second position is the classical one which still dominates present day religio-legal authorities. They stress that polygamy is here to stay and that the reason for not banning polygamy outrightly is rooted in the fact that there are special circumstances facing certain individuals and societies at certain times which make the limited practice of polygamy justifiable.[27] They maintain that the two verses explain the following:

(1) the institution of polygamy is basically upheld by the Quran;
(2) the status of polygamy in Islam is only a leave, a mere permission with restrictions put on it;
(3) the permission to practise polygamy was initially designed to protect widows and orphans 'as a social necessity and not for someone's fancy and indulgence';[28]
(4) although the above verse permits a man to marry more than one wife at a time, this permission is not without restrictions: first, he is strictly prohibited from abusing it, and 'to avail himself of it for merely sexual gratification is to misuse it';[29] secondly, before thinking of marrying a second wife, a man is instructed to ensure that he would be able to deal justly between his wives, and provide for them sufficiently. This implies that he should be able to give each of his wives an equal share in food, clothing, material comforts and whatever kind of treatment that he can provide. It also implies that he should not be partial to one wife at the expense of the other.[30] Aisha, one of the wives of the Prophet, relates that the Prophet gave each wife their due turn, was just to them, and used to pray to God thus: 'Oh Allah! I have fixed these turns and arrangements which are in my power; but for things that you alone can control, do not blame me'.[31] Hence it is justifiable for those men who have genuine reasons for it and who can deal with their wives equitably and look after them carefully.
(5) The kind of equality demanded by the Quran is one that is humanly attainable. Absolute equality is obviously not possible on the plane of human emotions and love. But a sincere attempt at treating one's

wives equally is possible; and equality is especially attainable in respect of these areas of life that are susceptible to control, such as companionship, provisions, and so on.[32]

THE LIMITATIONS IMPOSED ON THE PRACTICE OF POLYGAMY

Polygamy in Islam is permissible if it leads to justice and it is unlawful or forbidden if it results in grievances and injustices. So, dealing justly with one's wives is a religious obligation 'binding in conscience only and not as a legal restriction'.[33] However, dealing justly with one's wives is not an easy task to be achieved; only the exceptionally God-fearing can fulfil such a condition. Therefore, we are strongly of the opinion that the best way is to follow what the Quran recommends: 'If you fear that you will not do justice, then marry only one'.

The Quran is clear in stating that if there is fear of injustice, a man must be content with one wife only. This constitutes a moral and religious limitation on polygamy.[34] Besides, in order to protect women from being abused by men through the institution of polygamy, Islam has provided them with certain means of defence, which in themselves constitute a form of potential restriction on the practice of polygamy: first, a wife has the right to stipulate in her marriage contract that divorce would ensue if her husband contracts a second marriage;[35] second, the practice of polygamy is a voluntary course of action and is not to be imposed. Thus, if harm or injustice is done to a wife, she has the right to go to the judicial authorities for protection or divorce; third, a wife could also protect herself against the abuse of polygamy through the so-called 'delayed dowry', where a considerable amount of marriage endowment is held back to be claimed by the wife should a divorce take place.[36] In addition, in the *Hadith* literature there are certain moral exhortations which are interpreted as obstacles or hindrances to the practice of polygamy. For example, the Prophet is said to have declared God's condemnation of the 'sensual men and women'. When asked whom he meant, he replied: 'They are those who marry frequently in pursuit of carnal pleasures'.[37]

THE CONDITIONS UNDER WHICH POLYGAMY IS PERMITTED

As mentioned earlier, Islam prescribed monogamy as an ideal form of marriage. However, under exceptional circumstances the limited practice of polygamy is permitted. These circumstances are:[38] (1) the desire of a man to have children of his own if he discovers that his wife is unable to bear his children and therefore is unable to give him heirs. In this situation, polygamy would be more acceptable than for the man to divorce his barren wife for another. It is also not expected that a man should be deprived of his right to father children; (2) the desire of a man to marry a second wife if his first wife becomes critically ill and therefore incapable of fulfilling her duties as a wife. In this case, polygamy is far better than having a man divorce his sick wife when she needs him most. It is also more acceptable than the man having an extramarital affair behind his wife's back. The man should also not be expected to be celibate for the rest of his life; (3) as a social necessity when women outnumber men in the aftermath of a war. The outcome is not only women who cannot find husbands, but also more widows left without men to look after them.[39] Some add other reasons to the list which, in my opinion, have no legal foundation whatsoever in either the Quran or the Sunnah. Indeed, they do not make sense to the rational mind and reflect male egoism more than anything else. These conditions are said to be the following: (1) when the wife reaches old age and becomes weak and unable to look after her husband, he is then entitled to have a second wife; (2) if the wife has a bad character (from the husband's viewpoint) then he is allowed to contract a second marriage; (3) if the wife proved to be head-strong or disobedient; (4) when the husband supposedly possesses a strong sexual urge[40] and cannot do without a second wife.[41]

CONCLUSION

In Islam, polygamy is permitted under certain circumstances dictated in the Holy Quran. From the Islamic viewpoint, polygamy can benefit those involved on condition that the practice is regulated and not abused. This is believed to have been the case during early Islamic times. Its application, moreover, took place when circumstances necessitated it. However, today's reality is rather different. In the Muslim world, polygamy has been frequently abused.[42] On most occasions the Quranic injunctions are not implemented in their entirety (not only in the case of polygamy, but also in other issues related to women). Very often, the terms dictated by the Quran, are disregarded, if not wilfully contradicted, in order to benefit the males of the society. In these cases where a man has more than one wife, it can confidently be said that the majority of the men do not re-marry for the reasons stated in the Quran. Many times a man re-marries in his old age and chooses a young bride purely for the sake of feeling younger. So, to legitimise the relationship he will interpret the Quran as he wishes.

Another common reason given frequently by men is that the first wife is not capable of giving him sons, therefore he has to marry another woman in an attempt to produce a male heir. But the majority, especially the rich among them re-marry purely for self gratification. I myself know a man who brought his wife and two-year old daughter with him to England to study for a PhD. During his study (which lasted five years) the wife carefully looked after him and ensured that he would concentrate solely on his research project. By the time he finished his degree they all went back home; once they arrived he decided to have a second wife for no apparent reason but self-satisfaction. Another man came to Britain chiefly to look for a young Muslim girl who would be willing to marry him. When I asked him what was wrong with his existing wife he told me nothing. 'Why then do you want to have a second wife?' I asked. 'God allows us (men) to have more than one wife', he answered. 'What is the reaction of your wife?' I inquired. 'Positive. She gave me her permission to have a second wife', he explained. I wonder whether her approval came as a result of two difficult choices she had to make: either to accept the reality and share her husband with another woman or face an outright divorce. Although he insisted that his wife did not mind sharing him with another woman, I believe that she had no alternative but to capitulate.

The problem with this kind of man is that he does believe, mistakenly, that polygamy is his prerogative and that he could easily practise it whenever it suits him without due consideration to his existing marriage partner. There is no doubt that such Muslims have misused the option of polygamy granted to them by the Quran. In most cases those husbands neglect the senior wife or wives in preference to their young wife. Their children are also deprived of education, proper love, sympathy and care of their father. According to the Quran, all children are entitled to an equal share of the inheritance, but on many occasions fathers would sell their property to a favourite son in order to deprive other sons or daughters. In the Muslim world the typical polygamous family nowadays presents an unhappy and distorted picture that is very different from the one envisaged by the Quran.

The cause for the apparent disregard for the dictates of the Quran can be attributed to the fact that the character and conduct of the Muslims in general have deteriorated to the extent that the fear of Allah (which is, ultimately, the only effective guarantee of practising polygamy) and the sense of mutual obligation have almost disappeared. The Muslim countries are undergoing severe cultural alienation. Under such circumstances it is obvious that abuse of polygamy would occur frequently. This constitutes a serious problem not only for the family unit in society, but for society as a whole.

The position of Islam on polygamy is clear: a man is legally permitted to have up to four wives. However, this permission is restricted by the Quran's saying that justice must be done, and if a man fears injustice, he must be content with one wife only. Moreover, a man must remember that the practice is merely permission and is by no means encouraged. On the contrary, the Quranic decrees amount to a discouragement of polygamy unless certain conditions necessitate its practice (i.e. widows, orphans, no children from the first wife, etc.).

Given the fact that polygamy has been terribly abused and that it has brought misery on countless vulnerable women, it is important to stress that random or uncontrollable polygamy has be to stopped. In present day Muslim society, it is very difficult to leave this crucial issue to the individual conscience because there is no effective religious or moral deterrent. Therefore, the government must intervene in a way that would ensure the protection of women, particularly the vulnerable ones. This view is supported by the following statement by the former director of the Muslim Institute in Washington:

> 'An important point which has to be made clear in this context is that Islam gives the state the right to legislate rules which may at some point of time narrow down the degree of permissibility granted by the faith in the interest of society. No one questions the government's right to limit driving to one side of the road, or to forbid parking in certain places, or to prohibit the import or export of certain items, or building above a certain height. In the same way the legislature of a state may, if it is in the interest of its people, enact a law forbidding bigamy, a law which may be repealed after a war resulting in an excessive surplus of women, to protect them from descending to the most degrading profession'.[43]

Also, women, on their part, need to act against polygamy by refusing to become second, third or fourth wives when it is clearly wrong to do so. Very often women – or rather some women – enter willingly into polygamous relationships mainly for short-term benefits or expedients, thus allowing men to get away with the abuse. Men surely cannot be left free to contract multiple marriages whenever they like for the sake of their own self-indulgence. How can this be right? It is exploitative, and it is against the Divine decree.

Moreover, efforts to educate people about their rights and duties in society, as well as enlightening them with the knowledge of their religion, their aims and duties in life, are of crucial importance to prevent further abuse of this practice. In this respect, women in particular need to be made aware of their constructive role in society not only as wives and mothers but also as professionals in various disciplines. They should be encouraged to pursue knowledge, especially higher education, for polygamy will never survive in a society where there are a high number of educated and economically independent women. In so doing, women will be able to protect themselves as well as contribute positively to their societies rather than being locked in a social context defined by unhappy and disastrous marriages.

5 Female Circumcision: Religious Obligation or Cultural Deviation?

Throughout history female sexuality has provoked controversy and led to its being repressed in a variety of ways in all parts of the world. For example, the widows of deceased Pharaohs were buried alive to make sure that they would not be able to have relations with another man.[1] Also, it has been stated that in ancient Rome, female slaves had rings put through their labia majora to discourage them from getting pregnant. In twelfth-century Europe, chastity belts were widely used. Only one century ago, clitoridectomy was performed as a surgical remedy against masturbation in both Europe and the United States. Currently, cruel and inhumane genital surgery continues to take place in different parts of the world, a practice commonly known as female genital mutilation (FGM).[2]

Female genital mutilation is an age-old practice performed on the grounds of inherited convention rather than for health reasons. The operation is mostly done by a traditional circumciser, known as *daya*,[3] without anaesthetics, although recently it has been performed by some trained doctors and midwives. The practice involves cutting off parts of the whole organ of the female external genitalia.[4] The nature and scope of mutilation differ from one country to another. In certain countries the mutilation reaches its most extreme when the two sides of the wound are stitched together, leaving only a very small opening for menstrual blood. This form of mutilation is called infibulation and it is the most severe type of circumcision. It is estimated that over 80 million women and young girls have undergone genital mutilation world-wide and that some 5,000 girls each day are vulnerable to having genital mutilation carried out.[5]

The medical consequences of this practice are horrific. They range from chronic infections (as a result of the nature of, and procedures used in, the operation) to problems with childbirth, intercourse and menstruation. It is stated by the World Health Organisation (WHO) that female genital mutilation increases greatly the chance of the mother's death in childbirth and the risk of a child being born dead. Also, some girls who have undergone such an operation have lost their lives because of severe haemorrhaging resulting from shock due to excessive loss of blood.[6]

In recent years, female genital mutilation has received considerable publicity, especially in the West. Voices throughout the world have opposed it and started to call for urgent action to eradicate it: the American columnist A.M. Rosenthal branded it as 'the most widespread existing violation of human rights in the world' and suggested the halting of grants and loans to governments which allow it. In April 1994 the International Monetary Fund (IMF) made combatting female genital mutilation a condition for its loan to Burkina Faso. Due to the consistent efforts of the American novelist, Alice Walker,[7] many sanctuaries for mutilated women are now available in a number of countries.[8] President Clinton agreed in April 1994 to put the question of female genital mutilation on the agenda of American foreign policy.[9] Human rights groups are working hard to have female genital mutilation labelled as torture: 'Harm that is done to women is seen as a personal, private or cultural matter. Genital mutilation has not been seen as a type of harm', says Nancy Kelly, directing attorney of the women's refugee project;[10] and *Forward* (Foundation for Women's Health Research and Development) has described it as 'a violation of the fundamental human rights of the girl child' and 'another form of abuse under the guise of custom and tradition'.[11]

It has been said that FGM is rooted in religious and cultural traditions which makes it impossible to dislodge. So, does religion, or more specifically, Islam, advocate female genital mutilation? Does Islam – which condemned the Arab practice of female infanticide and elevated women spiritually and mentally and gave them the right to sexual pleasure – contradict itself and perpetuate this form of female subjugation? When I asked an Egyptian doctor, 'Why have you approved of female genital mutilation?' he answered that it was a religious obligation based on one of the sayings of the Prophet. When I demanded more elaboration, he, not surprisingly, failed to produce any tangible evidence.[12]

So, is female genital mutilation really an Islamic practice advocated by the Quran and the tradition? Or is it merely one of the old-fashioned customs which has infiltrated Islamic tradition and then later been assumed to be the expression of an Islamic principle? Before answering these questions, we need to look at the origin of the practice, its medical consequences, the reasons for it and its future prospects.

DEFINITION OF THE TERM

Female genital mutilation is a term used to describe a variety of genital operations performed on female children, young girls, and women. The operations are performed in the name of traditional beliefs and customs.

The nature, scope and severity of these operations vary from one country to another and from one area to another within the country itself. The age at which the mutilations are done range from a few days old to adolescence or adulthood. Upon performing the operation, celebration takes place to mark the occasion,[13] during which the girl receives presents and gifts. The celebration is supposed to have a social function – it indicates the willingness of the girl fully to enter into the community.[14]

Generally speaking, there are three main types of female genital mutilations:[15]

Circumcision. It is the mildest type of genital mutilation,[16] which involves cutting the prepuce or the hood of the clitoris. It is known in some Muslim countries as *Sunnah*, and it is the only form of mutilation which can accurately be described as circumcision; whereas there has been a tendency to refer to all forms of mutilation as circumcision.

Excision. This is the removal of the clitoris and either the entire labia minora, or a part of it.

Infibulation. This is the most severe form of mutilation. It consists of removing the whole of the clitoris, the labia minora and parts of the labia majora. The two sides of the vulva are then stitched together leaving a small hole for the discharge of menstrual blood and urine.

The operations themselves are carried out with special knives, with razor blades, or with pieces of glass. After the operation is done (especially with infibulation), the girl's legs are bound for 40 days to allow for healing and the formation of tissue.[17] It is important to stress that in some countries such as Sudan the first type of circumcision (the *Sunnah*) is used haphazardly to refer to other kinds of mutilation, most probably excision. In a recent survey which was conducted in North Sudan, it was found that 99 per cent of Sudanese women underwent one form or another of circumcision and that only 1 per cent had managed to escape the mutilation. Among the circumcised women, it was estimated that 2.5 per cent underwent *Sunnah* circumcision, 12.2 per cent excision and 85.3 per cent infibulation.[18]

THE ORIGIN OF THE PRACTICE

So far there has been no agreement on the origin of the practice. It has been suggested that female circumcision was widely practised in ancient Egypt; hence, it is thought that it was here that it first took place.[19]

However, it has also been suggested that the practice may be an old African puberty rite that was passed on to Egypt by diffusion. Moreover, it is assumed that it was a well-known practice in the pre-Islamic era in Egypt, Arabia and the Red Sea coasts. However, with the passage of time the practice survived in some areas and disappeared in others. Female genital mutilations are practised by Muslims, Catholics, Protestants, copts, animists, and non-believers in all countries concerned. In Egypt and Sudan, for example, both Muslims and Christians[20] practice female circumcision and the practice is encouraged on the grounds of custom and tradition. In Sudan, infibulation[21] is known as 'pharaonic circumcision', whereas in Egypt it is called Sudanese circumcision. Muslim people in some countries continue to believe mistakenly that non-circumcised women are unclean from a religious viewpoint, and that it is more hygienic and purer to have them circumcised.[22]

Currently, female genital mutilations are practised in more than 20 countries. In Africa,[23] it includes countries like Cameroons, Sierra Leone, Ghana, Mauritania, Chad, North Egypt, Kenya, Tanzania, Botswana, Mali, Sudan, Somalia, Ethiopia and Nigeria. In Asia, the practice is familiar among Muslims in the Philippines, Malaysia, Pakistan and Indonesia. In Latin America, female circumcision is practised in countries such as Brazil, Eastern Mexico and Peru. The practice also affects girls and women living in Western countries such as Britain, France, The Netherlands, Sweden, the United States, Australia and Canada (in these countries the practice is prohibited by law, but the mutilations take place clandestinely among immigrants who came from countries where the practice is prevalent). Female genital mutilations, moreover, are practised in the United Arab Emirates, South Yemen, Bahrain and Oman. However, these surgical operations are not common in countries like Saudi Arabia, Iran, Iraq, Jordan, Syria, Lebanon, Morocco, Algeria and Tunisia.[24]

THE ADVERSE EFFECTS OF CIRCUMCISION

Taking first the physical aspect of the problem, since these surgical operations are unnatural and carried out in unhealthy conditions, they are bound to have tremendous side-effects on the mutilated women. The most immediate complications are: pain, because these operations are very often done without the use of anaesthesia;[25] haemorrhaging to parts of the blood vessels such as the dorsal artery of the clitoris; panic and shock due to sudden and unexpected loss of blood; urinary retention;[26] urinary infection due to the use of unsterilised instruments and the kind of substances applied to the wound; fever, tetanus and blood poisoning due to the unhygienic conditions during the performance of the operations. Other severe consequences involve painful intercourse due to tight vaginal opening and difficulty in penetration;[27] lack of orgasm because of the cutting of the clitoris; prolonged and obstructed labour; frigidity; anxiety because of the failure to satisfy the husband's sexual and emotional needs.[28] One of my interviewees was a North Yemeni national who happened to be married (at the time of the interview) to a circumcised Egyptian woman. Shortly after the interview I was informed that their marriage had come to an end. The reason given was the failure of the wife to satisfy him sexually.[29] Menstrual complications are also often entailed by the surgical operation such as difficulty in passing menstrual blood. In some cases the blood is seriously prevented from being released because of tight circumcision. The blood then would accumulate and lead to increase in the size of the abdomen; vulval abscess and inclusion cysts.[30]

Also, there is a growing body of evidence that circumcision increases the chance of infection with human immunodeficiency virus (HIV).[31] It has been stated that allogeneic cells, that is, cells from an individual of the same species but of different genetic constitution, are the cause of AIDS; these allogeneic cells are sperm cells which induce the production of anti-sperm antibodies. Female circumcision, among other factors, allows sperm cells to be absorbed into the body and hence produce AIDS.[32]

THE REASONS GIVEN FOR FEMALE CIRCUMCISION

There are many reasons which have been given to justify the practice of female genital mutilation. But we will focus on the most familiar ones.[33] They are the following.

Hygienic Reasons. It is a common belief, among the communities concerned, that the external female genitals are dirty, and they are also considered ugly.[34] Hence, they need to be removed so as to maintain cleanliness and, it is alleged, to keep the skin smooth and hygienic. 'They are *Nigas*' (filthy) said one of the Sudanese interviewees and then added, 'It is clean and healthy to remove them'.[35] But it is hard to imagine how one would promote hygiene and cleanliness especially with infibulation, which is in itself a source of both infection and discomfort.

Sexual Reasons. This includes such issues as the preservation of virginity which is highly valued in all societies concerned, as it is a prerequisite for marriage. Hence, it is said that circumcision would protect and preserve the virginity of the young girls until the day they marry.[36] Another crucial issue very often mentioned by both women and men is the so-called 'over-sexed' nature of women and the need to reduce this desire so as to save them from shame and disgrace. 'It is important that all girls *be made to undergo circumcision* (my italics) so that they would keep their purity.' 'All our girls have to be circumcised – there is no exception.'[37] said an Egyptian nurse working in a medical centre in Sanaa. 'I agree with her – if I have a daughter I will definitely circumcise her – it is crucial that we attenuate our daughters' sexual desires and protect their chastity',[38] commented an Egyptian doctor working at the same medical centre.

Moreover, it has been argued that the rationale behind retaining the practice of female circumcision is to please or gratify the man. This is particularly the case with infibulation where it is thought that by narrowing the vaginal orifice man's sexual satisfaction will be maximised. Hence it is commonly held, among the communities concerned, that infibulation would keep or win over a husband.[39]

There is also frequent mention of the fact that circumcision would help polygamous men who have several wives to sexually satisfy them. It is strange how things have been distorted and taken out of their context. As I understand it one of the main aims of polygamy is to provide care for the widows and not to become a prerogative for males whereby they would use it to force women to undergo genital mutilation.

The Social Factor. This is centred on the question of whether or not the girl is socially accepted within the community, on which depends her reputation and eligibility for marriage. There is a widespread conviction, among the communities concerned, that an uncircumcised girl is bound to be talked about by people; her attitude would become corrupt, so it is argued, and she would start chasing men. This would consequently diminish her chances of marriage. This factor is so strong that sometimes even educated mothers are forced to circumcise their daughters in order to secure future marriage for them.[40]

When I was in Yemen, a Sudanese doctor informed me that an educated Jordanian mother (a pharmacist) came one day to her private practice asking for her daughter to be circumcised. The mother explained that her daughter's bad behaviour would jeopardise her chance of marriage.[41]

Religious Reasons. In the countries where female circumcision is practised, it is often justified on religious grounds. My main concern here is with Islam and female circumcision. Nearly all the Muslim groups concerned continue to believe – mistakenly – that circumcision is prescribed by the Islamic faith. For example, in countries such as Somalia, Egypt and Sudan, the practice is encouraged, perpetrated and even legalised (in the case of the *sunnah* circumcision in Sudan) as a required Islamic principle. Indeed, all the Egyptian nurses and doctors whom I interviewed stated that it was a religious duty, citing apparently one of the sayings of the Prophet Muhammad, in which he advised the traditional practitioner to be careful and not destroy the clitoris.[42]

HOW 'ISLAMIC' IS FEMALE CIRCUMCISION?

In order to be able to answer the question we need to look at the position of both the Quran and the Sunnah regarding the issue. The Quran is completely silent on the subject. This means that there is no divine commandment concerning the practice of female circumcision.[43] However, in the tradition or Sunnah apparently there exist a few *Hadiths* which allegedly recommend female circumcision. These are the following: the most often mentioned *Hadith* is the one in which the Prophet, having seen Umm Atiyyah – the circumciser, instructed her to 'cut slightly and do not overdo it because it is more pleasant for the woman and better for the husband';[44] 'circumcision is a Sunnah for the men and *Makrumah* (an honourable deed) for the women'; speaking to the Ansari women, the Prophet advised 'cut slightly without exaggeration because it is more pleasant for your husbands'; 'Female circumcision is a *makrumah*, and is there anything better than a *makrumah*?'.[45]

But a close look at these *Hadiths*[46] reveals that there are different and sometimes conflicting versions of them, which in the end undermine their credibility. Moreover, they are regarded, in general, as unauthentic and weak *Hadiths*: 'They are neither clear nor authentic', said Mahmud Shaltut, former sheikh of *al-Azhar* in Cairo.[47] Therefore, we can say, without hesitation, that female circumcision has no foundation in either the Quran or the Sunnah. Sheikh Abbas, Rector of the Muslim Institute at the Mosque in Paris affirms this view: 'If circumcision for the man (though not compulsory) has an aesthetic and hygienic purpose, there is no existing religious Islamic text of value to be considered in favour of female excision, as proven by the fact that this practice is totally non-existent in most of the Islamic countries. And if unfortunately some people keep practising excision, to the great prejudice of women, it is probably due to customs practised prior to the conversion of these people to Islam'.[48]

So the pretext that the practice of female genital mutilation is a religious obligation can easily be challenged and refuted. First, there is no direct or indirect reference in the Quran that sanctions or condones the practice of female circumcision.[49] Second, as for the traditions of the Prophet, they are regarded as inauthentic, unreliable and weak.[50] As such, they have no force or power for legislation.[51] This leads us to state that the practice has no Islamic foundation whatsoever. It is nothing more than an ancient custom which has been falsely assimilated to the Islamic tradition, and with the passage of time it has been presented and accepted (in some Muslim countries) as an Islamic injunction. Even the argument which states that there is an indirect correlation between Islam and the persistent retention of circumcision by virtue of the fact that Islam lays emphasis on issues such as seclusion, virginity, chastity, modesty and polygamy which trigger or add weight to the practice of mutilation[52] cannot be accepted, for one simple reason – why did these principles not encourage and perpetuate the practice in other Muslim countries where the custom is virtually unknown?

So, Islam does not enjoin circumcision and circumcision is not Islamic.[53] The practice is alien to both the ideals of Islam, and what one might call 'established' Islam. It is rather anti-Islamic, a form of human abuse; it is harmful and the only possible demand is for it to be stopped immediately.[54]

As for how to eradicate this form of abuse – this will depend on both domestic and international efforts. Domestically, the governments in the countries concerned should enhance, through education, the awareness of both males and females of the following: first, the medical risks involved in continuing such practices; second, the fact that the custom has no religious grounds and therefore is not a religious duty. The role of the religious leaders could be extremely effective because of their immense influence on ordinary people, especially in the rural areas where the practice is still prevalent. Muslim scholars are obliged to adopt a positive attitude towards the issue and participate seriously in the process of abolishing the practice. They need, urgently, to reach a unanimous and clear verdict in which they would clarify once and for all the genuine position of Islam regarding the tradition: that female circumcision is not part of authentic Islam and that true Islam would never condone such an inhumane and destructive practice.

So far, the majority of them have unfortunately shown great reluctance and unwillingness to cooperate. On the contrary, some of them have been very hostile to the idea of abandoning the habit. This became clear when, in April 1995, *al-Azhar* issued a *fatwa*[55] expressly allowing the continuation of the custom to take place in Egypt. Immediately afterwards, the Egyptian health minister issued a statement in which he stressed that the practice is deeply rooted in Egyptian culture and that 90 per cent of Egyptian families still practise it. Therefore, from his viewpoint, it is inconceivable to eradicate it, thus making it difficult for the advocates to find any support or welcoming ground among ordinary people.[56] Also, the governments should encourage and support parents who refuse to circumcise their daughters, thus helping them to withstand social pressure.

Internationally, the international bodies and interested people can lend their help to the local authorities in the countries concerned to overcome the obstacles which could hinder their efforts toward the total abolition of this practice. However, this help should be given in such a way that the communities concerned would not react with outright resentment of foreign interference. The issue is very sensitive and it needs careful handling. Sensational statements will only be counter productive. Female circumcision, after all, is a culturally-rooted practice and it will not disappear overnight. People, especially when their mores or way of life come under attack from outsiders, tend to cling to these values and try to protect them even if some of these cultural values or practices do not make sense to the rational mind. So the best way to achieve genuine change is to approach the issue with patience, openness, and due consideration to the positive aspects of the value system in question. The aim, in other words, should be to enable the communities concerned to undergo specific process of reform, without their entire system of values being questioned, denigrated or rejected.

6 Islam and Women's Inheritance

One of the crucial changes brought about by Islam was the establishment of the principle of women's right to inheritance. It constituted a radical departure from pre-Islamic practices which not only denied women any right to inherit, but actually treated them as though they themselves were objects to be inherited.

The chapter of the Quran called 'The Women' (*al-Nisa*) details in a just manner the share of inheritance that is due to each individual, male and female. According to this chapter, women are not only no longer allowed to be inherited like chattels but, as individuals, they have a legal right to inheritance. 'Men shall have a share in what their parents and kinsmen leave; and women shall have a share in what their parents and kinsmen leave; whether it be little or much, it is legally theirs'.[1] This verse was revealed when an Ansari woman came to the Prophet and complained that after her husband's death she and her daughter were prevented from inheriting any of his property. Her husband's brother justified the action by stating that, 'Women do not mount horses, do not endanger themselves and go into battle', therefore they could not be allowed to inherit.[2]

Before the revelation of the above-cited verse, inheritance was the prerogative of men only; women had no say or role in the matter. 'When a man passed away, his eldest son inherited his father's widow. He could then, if she was not his real mother, either marry her or ask his brother or his nephew, if he so wishes, to marry her in his place.'[3] Before Islam, women were not only deprived of their right to inheritance, but also had no impact over their own destiny, which was a matter between the men of the husband's clan or her own relatives. During the *Jahiliyya*, when a man lost his father, brother, or son, and that person left a widow, the heir, taking advantage of the fact that her dowry was paid by the dead man, rushed to the widow, covered her with his cloak, thus claiming (unjustly) to himself the sole right to marry her. When he married her, he denied her of her right to the part of the inheritance constitued by the dowry. But if he decided, for one reason or another, not to have her as a wife, he could then ask another person to marry her. In return he would take (for himself) her dowry. However, if the widow (at the time of her husband's death) managed to

61

get to her own clan before the arrival of the heir, he would lose his rights over her in favour of the males of her own clan.[4]

The new laws regarding women challenged the social structure of a society that had given males the upper hand over females in matters related to inheritance. Therefore, it was inevitable that it would create an uproar among sections of the male population who felt threatened by them and questioned the validity of granting women a share in the inheritance. So, they decided to ignore these laws and continued to apply the customs of the *Jahiliyya*, hoping that as time went by the Prophet would change them. But the matter was brought to the surface by women themselves who continued to suffer from the *Jahiliyya* mentality. Kubaysha bint Ma'an went to the Prophet and complained that the new laws were not put into practice, because her son-in-law denied her her right to inheritance. 'Messenger of God', she appealed, 'I have neither taken my share of inheritance from my husband, nor been left alone to enjoy my freedom and re-marry.'[5] The Prophet's answer to her son-in-law and other hypocrites in Arabia was sharp and clear. He recited the following verses:

> O believers, it is unlawful for you to inherit the women of your deceased kinsmen against their will, or to bar them from re-marrying in order that you may force them to give up a part of what you have given them, unless they be guilty of a proven crime[6]

This verse answered not only Kubaysha's appeal but also aimed at eradicating the *Jahiliyya* customs that were prevailing in Arabia. Inheritance among the people of Yathrib (Medina) was as follows: when a man died, his son automatically inherited his stepmother. She could not challenge this arrangement. He could marry her if he so wished and have with her the same relations as his father had had before him; or he could leave her if he was no longer interested in her. When the heir was too young, the widow (stepmother) was stopped from re-marrying and forced to wait until the heir became mature enough to take a decision concerning her future.[7] In Mecca, the situation regarding women was even worse: the (*Aidl*) (imprisonment) was common among the Quraysh in Mecca. A man married a noble woman. If he disliked her, he separated from her after securing an agreement with her that she would only re-marry with his approval. To validate the agreement, the husband would bring witnesses and in their presence put the terms of the agreement in a written contract. If a person wanted to marry that woman, she would not be able to make any decision concerning her future without the permission of her former husband. And in order to win his approval she had to pay him a sum of money big enough to satisfy him. Otherwise he could easily oppose and stop it.[8]

Married women were not the only ones to fall victim to constant threat and blackmail. Young girls too, especially fatherless girls, were in the same situation, if not worse. For pre-Islamic Arabian society, it was outrageous to allow fatherless children (of both sexes) who could not fight or earn a living to have shares in the inheritance. Therefore, they were denied any rights to inheritance. Moreover, they were mistreated and not looked after well, especially young girls who were also the object of sexual abuse. For example, the guardian very often decided to marry the prettiest ones, thus securing two things for himself: (1) controlling their share of inheritance; (2) getting away from or escaping paying a dowry for them. If a fatherless girl happened to be ugly or not pretty enough to persuade him to marry her, he would use her ugliness to oppose any marriage for her. In doing so, he did not have to pay her share of inheritance. 'If a fatherless girl was ugly, her guardian did not give her her share. He forced her not to marry and waited for her to pass away so that he would assume control over her inheritance.[9]

But Islam, with its egalitarian message which aimed at redressing the injustice of society, would not tolerate such inhumane practices. It began by affirming the legal right of fatherless children to have a share in their own inheritance and ended by cautioning against depriving them of their due. It would be useful to look carefully at the following verses, all of which condemned the practices as inhumane and warned of grave consequences if they be continued:

Give orphans the property which belongs to them. Do not exchange their valuables for worthless things or devour their possessions, adding them to yours; for this would surely be a great sin.[10]

Put orphans to the test till they reach a marriageable age. If you find them capable of sound judgement, hand over to them their property, and do not deprive them of it by squandering it before they come of age.[11]

Those that devour the property of orphans unjustly, swallow fire into their bellies; they shall burn in the flames of fire.[12]

They will ask you about alms-giving. Say: whatever you bestow in charity must go to your parents and to your kinsfolk, to the orphan and to the poor man and to the wayfarer. Allah is aware of whatever good you do.[13]

And again:

Serve Allah and associate none with Him. Show kindness to your parents and your kindred, to the orphans and to the needy, to your near and distant neighbours, to your fellow-travellers, to the wayfarers, and to the slaves whom you own. Allah does not love arrogant and boastful men, who are themselves niggardly and enjoin others to be niggardly also; who conceal that which Allah of His bounty has bestowed upon them – we have prepared a shameful punishment for the unbelievers – and who spend their wealth for the sake of ostentation, believing neither in Allah nor in the Last Day. He that chooses the devil for his friend, an evil friend has he.[14]

Do not touch the property of orphans, but strive to improve their lot until they reach maturity. Give just weight and full measure; we never charge a soul with more than it can bear. Speak for Justice, even if it affects your own kinsmen.[15]

The above verses were beyond the comprehension of those who were unable to assimilate the full import of the changes brought about by Islam. 'How' they say 'can one grant children and women the right to inheritance? Is it possible to allow women and children who do not earn money to have shares in the inheritance? How can an ugly, fatherless girl have the right to a share in the inheritance?' They were puzzled, bewildered and confused by the whole situation. First, they decided to wait, hoping for rectification from Heaven. When that wish did not materialise, they turned to the Prophet, seeking clarification. The Prophet never felt threatened by them; on the contrary, his answer was straightforward: stop being muddle-headed. God has informed you of his decision on this issue, and all you need to do is to comply with His Divine instruction.[16] He then went on, reciting the following verse:

They consult you concerning women. Say, Allah has instructed you about them, and so has the Book, which has been proclaimed to you, concerning the orphan girls whom you deny their lawful rights and refuse to marry; also regarding helpless children. He has instructed you to deal justly with orphans. Allah has knowledge of all the good you do.[17]

In order to block any future attempts by the hypocrites to deny women their rights to inheritance, verses continued to be revealed to the Prophet affirming the same message and explaining in detail the share of each individual in all possible conditions.

You shall inherit the half of what your wives leave if they die childless. If they leave children, a quarter of what they leave shall be yours after payment of any bequest they may have bequeathed or debt. Your wives shall inherit one quarter of what you leave if you die childless. If you leave children, they shall inherit one eighth, after payment of any bequest you may have bequeathed, or debt. If a man or a woman leave neither children nor parents and have a brother or a sister, they shall each inherit one-sixth. If there be more, they shall equally share the third of the estate, after payment of any bequest that may have been bequeathed or debt without prejudice (to the right of the heirs). This is a commandment from Allah. He is Gracious and all-Knowing.[18]

In making these provisions, Islam has firmly established and secured forever the legal right of women to have a share in inheritance.

However, it has been stated that although Islam granted woman the right to inheritance, her share is by no means fair and equal to that given to man. The critics refer to the verse that allows the brother to take twice as much as the share of their sisters. (4: 10) Therefore, they view this as detrimental to the dignity of women. By giving women half the share of men, they say, there is a clear implication that women are inferior to men. This argument has been used by both Muslims and non-Muslims. But it is based on a fallacy. If it happens for one reason or another that one sex receives a greater or lesser share than the other, this does not mean that the recipient of the lesser share is regarded as inferior. The whole issue of inheritance in Islam depends entirely on the social and economic context, and the role or function of a particular sex within it. If this crucial contextual factor is borne in mind, a proper understanding of the verses related to inheritance in the Quran would ensue.[19] Let us first read the verse mentioned above which defines the different shares in the property of a deceased person. It states:

Allah has thus enjoined you concerning your children. A male shall inherit twice as much as a female. If there be more than two girls, they shall have two thirds of the inheritance; but if there be one only, she shall inherit the half. Parents shall inherit a sixth each if the deceased has a child; but if he has no children and his parents be his heirs, his mother shall have a third. If he has brothers, his mother shall have a sixth after payment of any bequest he may have bequeathed, or debt. You know not whether your parents or your children are more beneficial to you. But this is the law of Allah; He is Wise and All-knowing.[20]

The context in which the verse was revealed took place when an Ansari woman came to the Prophet and informed him that her husband had passed away and left her with five daughters. His male relatives, instead of helping her, had taken all his wealth, leaving her and her daughters with nothing to fall back on. The answer to her complaint was that the Prophet recited this verse and accordingly gave her and her five daughters their share of the inheritance.[21]

Now if we read this verse in conjunction with other verses related to inheritance and analyse them carefully, we see that women in the last analysis are beneficiaries, or at least they are not worse off. In what way? Firstly, the Quran has ensured that women could get their shares of inheritance not only as daughters, but also as mothers and wives. Secondly, the fact that women have been given half the share of male heirs has to be looked at within its social and economic framework. In Islam the wife is to be cared for by her husband, even if she is wealthy enough to maintain herself. By law she is entitled to claim maintenance from her husband. At the same time she is not obliged to spend any of her wealth on the household. In addition a Muslim woman receives at the time of her marriage a considerable sum of money. This money, which the husband is obliged to pay, constitutes her dowry, or *Mahr*, which belongs to her alone. She is free to use, spend or invest it in any way she likes. Therefore, as a wife she adds to whatever she receives through inheritance in her capacity as daughter and that, too, without any legal commitment to support either herself or her children.[22]

Let us hear what the Ikhwan al-Safa (leading Muslim intellectuals of their time) had to say about the issue of female inheritance in Islam:

> Brother, many of the intellectuals who engage themselves in the study of philosophy and metaphysics, when they reflect with their rationality upon the Divine Laws and compare them with their own thoughts, directions and understanding, their judicious acumen (*ijtihad*) and comparative reasoning (*qiyas*) lead them to feel that most of the Divine prescriptions appear to be against justice, truth and rectitude. All this is because of their deficiency in understanding, paucity of discretion and lack of knowledge about the essence of the secrets of the Divine Law. For example, when they reflect upon the rule of inheritance that a male will have twice the share of a female, they feel that the correct position should have been the female getting twice the portion of a male. For women are feeble and have no venues for earning money. They (the intellectuals) do not know and understand that the rule laid down in the Divine Law actually leads to what they hint at and desire for. For example, if you were to inherit from your father one thousand dirhams, and your sister 500 dirhams, at her marriage she will take another 500 dirhams as a dowry, making her share one thousand; whereas when

you marry you will give 500 dirhams as dowry that shall leave with you half of what your sister has received. In this manner, the Divine Law would produce the result they have desired and hinted at. This is the manner in which you should look at the Divine Law so that the exact rectitude and substance of truth may become apparent. One should be aware that the insight of the Law-Giver in the requirements of his laws is not a partial and fragmentary insight, for the benefits of some and to the exclusion of others, or for the ready present (transitoriness) to the exclusion of the future (eternity), but it is an absolute insight aiming at the good and rectitude of all, for the present as well as the future.[23]

As is clear from the above argument, the position of women is secure as far as inheritance is concerned. Although women have been given half the share of men, their financial situation in the long term is guaranteed. This is due to the fact that the marriage contract gives her the right to ask for *Mahr* (which is usually substantial) as well as claim maintenance, both of which entail no legal commitment to anybody including herself. But it may be objected, what about women who cannot marry for one reason or another? What about the ones who cannot work and earn a living, especially in the rural areas where women have been denied the chance to gain a decent education? How would they live and maintain themselves? These exceptional cases can be dealt with as follows:

Firstly, the Quranic injunctions make it clear that male relatives, especially brothers, have the obligation to care for women and meet their financial needs. At the moment, in most Muslim countries this issue has been left to the individual conscience, which has led to many cases of abuse and desertion. Therefore, in order to secure and protect these women, governments need to legislate and make it legally binding on those male relatives to pay for the upkeep of their needy women.

Secondly, the Quran makes it clear that a person is entitled to make a will. Indeed, it is highly recommended by the Prophet that a person should prepare a will as early as possible and not wait until it is too late. Contrary to the misconception held by large sections of the Muslim public that a person has no right to make a will, both the Quran and the Sunnah encourage people to do so. There are even some misguided jurists who argue, contrary to clear principles in the Quran, that Islam does not recommend the making of wills. This negative attitude advocated by a small band of jurists has confused ordinary Muslim people and has led many to abandon the idea of making wills. Hence, at present we see that the majority of Muslims do not think seriously of wills, let alone making ones of their own. The Quran, on the other hand, has specifically asked for the distant relatives, the needy people and the orphans to be treated kindly and to be helped if they are present at the time of the division of inheritance:

> If relatives, orphans, or needy men are present at the division of an inheritance, give them, too, a share of it, and speak to them in kind words.[24]

So, if the Quran is so kind even to distant relatives and needy people by virtue of the fact that it encourages people to give them some share of the inheritance, I see no problem, in keeping with this spirit of Divine Justice, that a bequest be made in favour of a needy person, particularly if this person is a close member of the family. The point here is emphasised that if parents think that their daughter is unable to get married for whatever reason and she is in a disadvantaged position, they can write a will in her favour in order to secure her future. This accords with the spirit of the Quran and the Sunnah. The Prophet is reported to have said: 'It is better to leave your inheritors well off than destitute'.[25]

Theoretically speaking, then, the position of Muslim women as far as inheritance is concerned is secure and guaranteed by the Islamic Law. But in practice this is not the case. Constantly, the Divine instructions concerning women's rights to inheritance are violated and overlooked by Muslim societies. Social, political, economic and cultural factors play a major role in determining who does and who does not take a share. In such situations the weak (in this case, women) have always been kept at bay when it comes to their right to inheritance. This takes place in both the cities as well as the rural areas. Very often, strong social pressure is applied on women to renounce their shares for the benefit of the immediate male members of the family. This is particularly the case when women are well off or married to wealthy men. Their due is automatically written off and transferred to their male relatives. Whether they like it or not they are all too often forced to accept the loss of their shares; if they refuse, they are accused of being selfish, greedy, inconsiderate and irresponsible. Often this has led to tension, friction and conflict of interests among the members of the family, shattering the whole concept of caring and sharing which lies at the heart of the Islamic faith. Here are a few examples which illustrate the evident disregard for the Divine decrees regarding women's right to inheritance. These examples are by no means confined only to this particular area (the Azad Kashmir area of Pakistan), but are part of a wider phenomenon to be found throughout the Islamic world:

Case 1: Abdullah, a wealthy father aged 85, died leaving behind two daughters and a son (Muhammad), all of them married with children of marriageable age. During his lifetime, Abdullah neither divided the inheritance nor left a will. As the daughters of Abdullah were married, it was assumed (by their brother Muhammad and the community) that there was no need for them to claim their share of the inheritance. Hence Muhammad took over the estate and the sisters were forced to accept the harsh reality of giving up their due. A year later, Muhammad suddenly passed away, leaving behind four sons and three daughters. Again, the daughters (like their aunts beforehand) were prevented from asking for their entitlements, while the four sons were given the right to take over the entire inheritance. As the daughters of Muhammad were not married, this situation put them at the mercy of their four brothers in terms of maintenance and welfare.

Case 2: Ibrahim and Fatima were a well-educated, married couple, who died at the ages of 90 and 85 respectively. Ibrahim died first and left his inheritance to his wife, three sons and a daughter, to be divided according to Islamic Law. However, the daughter decided not to take her share of the inheritance. When she was asked for the reasons, she replied stating the following:

1. She felt that if she had to claim her due she would lose the respect and love of her brothers (because of the stigma attached to the issue of women daring to claim their shares). Because it is customary in Pakistan that sisters would never ask for their shares of inheritance, she feared that by claiming her due, the community would degrade her and look down upon her.

2. She took into consideration the feeling of her sister-in-law, who would neither like her nor support her had she asked for her entitlement (in Pakistan, as elsewhere in the Muslim world, sisters-in-law are regarded as the real inheritors (through their husbands) of the wealth of the elderly father-in-law and in this case it was the wealth of father-in-law Ibrahim).

3. Financially speaking, she thought that she was not in a desperate situation and therefore there was no need to rock the boat.

Case 3: Fazel and Aisha were a married couple who had six children: two sons and four daughters. Fazel suddenly died at the young age of 42, leaving behind his widow with six children in a difficult situation. Their only source of livelihood was a small piece of land which Fazel had left; therefore, the land was kept undivided so that the eldest son would work on it in order to provide a source of income for the rest of the family. As time went by, the sons and daughters got married one by one. Also, the two sons had the opportunity to go to Britain and start work and ended up earning good money. For many years, the small piece of land which the father had left behind was forgotten. However, at a certain stage the daughters of Fazel (sensing that everybody was doing well) decided that the time was right to claim their shares of the land. The demand caused a great family feud. The sisters were accused of being greedy and selfish even though they were entitled to their shares according to the Islamic Law. However, after a long and protracted struggle, the sisters got their due, but this came at the expense of their relations with their brothers.

The above examples show that the Islamic concept of broad and equitable shares which take into consideration the interests of all persons concerned has been transferred into a prerogative for males, outrageously disregarding[26] the Divine Will. There is no doubt about the fact that in most parts of the Muslim world the Islamic Law concerning women's rights to inheritance is not in operation; instead it is social and cultural rules which dominate. It is crucial that something has to be done to rectify this situation, and women themselves have an essential role to play in the process of any such change. They have to stand up against these violations and try to be more active and effective in order to reclaim their right to their own inheritance; there is no use in being passive. Determined action on the part of all suffering Muslim women is the only path that will yield any fruit.

7 The Dissolution of Marriage in Islam

Although in most societies divorce is met with social disapproval, nonetheless it is a natural and inevitable phenomenon in human society. Hence, we find that in every society there are ways and means which allow the marital link to be dissolved if it fails to fulfil its objective.

The reasons for the dissolution of marriage are, generally speaking, common and almost universal. According to the research of Abd al-Ati, they 'apply to human society – irrespective of time, place or level of civilisation (and they range) from the unavoidable death of a spouse or involuntary barrenness to the trivial cooking mistake of burning the husband's food or putting too much salt in it, not to mention the man's arbitrary dislike of his spouse or capricious preference for another woman who seems more pleasing to him.'[1]

So the termination of marriage is sometimes inevitable and no system can afford to ignore this reality, otherwise it is doomed to failure. Any system which insists on the indissolubility of marriage and overlooks the fact that under exceptional circumstances the dissolution of the family becomes a necessity is static, impractical and does not respond adequately to human needs.

Most importantly, a system under which marriage is indissoluble would inevitably lead to the abuse of marriage, because people will always find ways around it, hence defeating the whole purpose which the system stands for in the first place: that is, to prevent the marital tie from being dissolved.

An Attitude that Allows but Discourages

Islam allows divorce but *only* under extraordinary circumstances. In principle, Islam regards marriage as a life-long commitment. However, sometimes there do arise situations wherein marriage ceases to fulfil its purpose. Hence, divorce can be invoked by either side or both of them in order to accommodate the realities of an unsuccessful marriage. It must be stressed that divorce can only be exercised as the last resort after all efforts for reconciliation between the spouses are exhausted. Therefore, in Islam divorce is considered a necessity if the married partners are not happy.

71

However, divorce is heavily disapproved of and discouraged. The Quran discourages divorce in the following verses: 'And (remember) when you (Muhammed) said to the man (Zayd, Muhammed's adopted son) whom Allah and yourself have favoured: keep your wife and have fear of Allah'.[2] In this verse there is an implicit disapproval of divorce. In other verses the Quran clearly discourages Muslims from having recourse to a hasty divorce, even though they might be dissatisfied with their marriage partners. 'Treat them with kindness; for even if you do dislike them, it may well be that you may dislike a thing which Allah has meant for your own good'.[3] The Quran not only discourages divorce, but it prohibits the slandering of one's wife in order to take back her dowry 'If you wish to have a wife in the place of a (divorced) one, do not take from her the dowry you have given her even it if be a talent of gold. That would be improper and grossly unjust; for how can you take it back when you have lain with each other and entered into a firm contract?'[4]

Divorce was also discouraged by the Prophet, who is reported to have said: 'Of all things licit, the most hateful to God is divorce.'[5] Also: 'Let not the faithful man hate the faithful woman; if he dislikes some of her habits, he may like others.'[6] Ali, the son-in-law of the Prophet, said, 'Marry and do not divorce your wives, for divorce causes God's throne to tremble.'[7]

These disapprovals notwithstanding, Islam concedes the possibility of divorce as the lesser of two evils when the alternative is a disastrously unhappy marriage and it devotes much attention to dealing with it both in the Quran as well as in the Sunnah. For example, the Quran has devoted to divorce an entire chapter, which bears the same name (*Surat al-talaq*). In addition, there are many other verses throughout the Quran that deal with the subject.

Islam adopts the principle that married couples should not be forced to remain in a union which they find intolerable, and which causes them great distress and unhappiness.

Reasons why Spouses might want Divorce

From the Islamic viewpoint, there are many causes for divorce: if the spouses discover that they are incompatible because of their ideas and opinions, their modes of behaviour and their temperaments, then they should resort to divorce. The conflict and tension that would inevitably arise as a result of their incompatibility would certainly give rise to ill-feeling and contempt between the spouses. This would adversely affect not only the couple but their children (if they have any) as well as their relatives and closest friends. As a way out of this difficult situation, Islam therefore prescribes divorce. Furthermore, spouses locked forcibly in an unhappy union would surely be forced themselves – in an attempt to satisfy their sexual urge – to seek sexual intimacy outside the marriage tie, hence falling into the trap of committing adultery, which is forbidden in Islam. To prevent partners from indulging in such indecency, Islam allows the couple to be divorced so that they can go their own separate ways. Divorce is also granted if the husband is impotent (here it must be stressed that although women have grounds for divorce in this case they are, generally speaking, under strong social – not religious – pressure not to make use of it. I know at least two women who are living with impotent husbands but they cannot venture to seek divorce); or if the wife is barren (the husband, in this case, can easily and with social blessing, dismiss and divorce his wife if he discovers that she is unable to bear him children). Divorce, moreover, can take place if both spouses or one of them suffers a serious disease that renders the continuation of the marital relation either impossible or unsafe, or if the husband is put in prison for a long time or fails to support his wife (financially). In such cases, divorce may occur, but only as a last resort.[8]

Regarding the etymology of the word '*talaq*', the English word 'divorce' is very often interpreted to mean *talaq* and vice-versa; this translation, however, is misleading. For the word 'divorce' 'traces its origin back to the Latin derivative and conjures up the splitting of a unit, the permanent physical separation of the spouses', while the Arabic word '*talaq*' is derived from the verb *itlaq* which means to set loose, set free or to leave. *Talaq*, therefore, within the context of the marital link means to terminate (*as in free one from*) the bond created by a marriage contract. Hence the word dissolution might be more appropriate than divorce in this context.[9]

Pre-conditions for Divorce

In order for the divorce (or more properly the dissolution of the marriage contract) to be effective and valid, the person who is performing it has to be adult (*baligh*), sane (*aqil*), free from any confusion or coercion and full of clear and good intentions (*qasid*). In addition, the witnesses have to be reliable, trustworthy and of good conduct.[10]

Divorce in Islam is one of those issues which has generated considerable controversy and debate among Muslims and non-Muslims alike; this is probably because it has been grossly abused by Muslims and certainly misunderstood by both Muslims and non-Muslims. But first, let us see what the Quran has to say about the dissolution of the marital tie.

The Quran and the Issue of Divorce: Arbitration Method

Islam is against divorce and is strongly in support of the family unit: hence, both spouses have to do their utmost to build up a strong and harmonious marital relationship. If, however, tension arises between them, they should not rush into a hasty divorce. First, they should try and make some serious efforts to save their marriage. For example, they should attempt to understand the causes of their differences and try to solve them in a private and amicable way. If this proves to be unsuccessful, then they are advised to ask representatives, one from each side, to mediate and try to restore peace between them. The Quran says, 'If you fear a breach between a man and his wife, appoint an arbiter from his people and another from hers. If they wish to be reconciled, Allah will bring them together again – Allah is Knowing, Wise'.[11] The arbiters have to be close to the parties involved and command their trust and respect. They should conduct their task impartially and discreetly. Also, they should try and settle the differences between the spouses without publicity; they should especially attempt to avoid the embarrassment of revealing such issues that might be regarded (by the married partners) as very private and intimate. The decisions reached by the arbiters are binding on both spouses. However, if one or both of them refuse to abide by them, then the rulings have to be enforced by the court. Here, it must be noted that the Quran clearly protects the right of the woman in this matter. By insisting here that *two* arbiters one from the side of each party (the husband as well as the wife) have to be called to investigate the matter between them peacefully and objectively, it has in fact put the interests of the wife on an equal footing with those of her husband, by giving her the opportunity to present her case and viewpoint before the arbiters. This is surely a fair and just way to deal with divorce matters because it takes into consideration the interests of both sides. More importantly, it protects the weak (the wife) from being abused by the strong (the husband) an outcome which all too frequently occurs in our society these days. For example, it prevents the husband from arbitrarily divorcing his wife without any due consideration for her mental or physical well-being, a practice very often used by the husband to punish his wife in contemporary Muslim societies. Also, mediation is more humane and civilised, since it allows spouses more time to think and reflect on their situation and alert them to the possible consequences of hasty and unconsidered decisions.

Historical and Constitutional Examples

In light of the above it would seem sensible to favour and recommend the adoption of this orderly divorce process by the judicial systems of all

Muslim countries (some of them have already adopted this process – in Tunisia, for example, section 30 of the Law enacting that: Divorce outside a court of Law is without Legal effect[12]), for it is simple, civilised and, most importantly, authentically Islamic: it has been described and recommended by the Quran. So, it is not something foreign or alien to Islam; on the contrary, it is an integral part of the Islamic tradition. Indeed there are many examples in which divorce cases were judged according to this procedure in early Islamic history. For instance, it has been reported that during the reign of the fourth Caliph Ali (son-in-law of the Prophet), a man and his wife approached him complaining about each other's behaviour and stating that there were gross differences between them that had made their lives miserable. Ali immediately acted as Judge and asked for representatives from both sides to be despatched to him. Upon their arrival, he commissioned them to look into the matter carefully and decide whether there would be any possibility of making peace between them. Also, he reminded them of their responsibility and sacred duty to handle the case with tact, due consideration and impartiality. He told them that if they sensed that there was a chance that they could be reconciled then they should spare no effort in doing so, otherwise they had to be separated with honour and in dignity. When the arbiters reached a decision, Ali made it legally effective by forcing the spouses to abide by it.[13] It must be stressed here that Ali's act in this case was perfectly in accordance with the directive contained in Chapter 4, verse 34 and with the overall spirit of the message of the Quran which aims, in its essence, at achieving gender equality. His understanding of the rules of the verse in question is shared by other eminent companions. Al-Tabari, for example, commenting on this verse stated the following: Ibn Jarir reported from Ibn Abbas saying: This (the verse in question) is when a rift arises between husband and wife. God orders them to appoint representatives, one from each side, so that they would investigate the disputed matter. If the arbiters, after a thorough examination, find out that the husband is the guilty one, then they have power to set her free and force him to pay her compensation. But if they discover that the wife is the cause of the problem, they are authorised to advise her and deprive her of any payment. However, if the arbiters realise that there is a good chance for patching up things between the spouses, they are encouraged to do so, but if they think otherwise, the partners have to be allowed to go their own separate ways.[14]

It is most unfortunate that such a humane understanding of the verse and such a civilised practice of it (as was the case with Ali) failed to materialise throughout most of our Islamic history. For one reason or another, both the jurists as well as the rulers decided to ignore and shelve it. Nevertheless, there were a few scholars who continued to stress the importance of utilising the directions contained in this verse and use them as guidance to promote legal or judicial divorce systems in the Muslim world. One of the most respected Egyptian scholars, Muhammed Abduh, advocated such reform. In his book *Women and Islam*, Abduh explains Chapter 4, verse 35 as follows: The call in this verse [if you fear a breach between a man and his wife, appoint an arbiter from his people and another from hers] is a general, not specific, one. It cannot be the responsibility of every person or every group of people in society. Therefore, there are two opinions among the interpreters: one says that the call (in the verse) is directed to the people who are concerned with the genral affairs of the Muslim people, namely the rulers or representatives who are responsible for their overall well being. The second opinion, however, insists that the general call includes also the spouses and their relatives. Hence, if the married couple or their relatives succeed in solving the dispute and making peace between them, then this is fine; otherwise other learned Muslims have to help in this matter.

Abduh continues: both opinions are right, for the first one allocates the responsibility of looking after the interest of the people in the hands of the representatives who have to endeavour to do their jobs properly, while the second one assigns the duty to the general public who have to team up and be cooperative with one another. As far as the representatives are concerned, Abduh explains that there are two different views: one sees that the arbiters as mere mediators with no legal authority, while the other insists on regarding them as judges with legal power to enforce their decisions. Concerning the part which states, 'If they wish to be reconciled, Allah will bring them together again. Allah is Knowing, Wise', Abduh interprets it thus: this part means that God favours peace and harmony between spouses and wishes that they would be reconciled, because of the emphasis Islam lays on the family unit in society. As such, the arbiters are exhorted to ensure that peace can prevail between them. However, if the arbiters fail to bridge the gap between the couple, they are not to blame.[15] Abduh then introduces his own version. He says: when conflict erupts between husband and wife and proves difficult to solve amicably, the spouses are advised to take the matter to the judge of the county (meaning to the court). The judge here has to appoint two mediators – one represents the wife while the other acts for the husband. Both representatives have to be of good character and highly respected people. The judge, after briefing them, has to send them to the spouses in an attempt to solve the dispute. If the arbiters' efforts culminate in success, then it is good news. But if they fail to bring the two spouses together again, then they have the legal power to divorce them. The representatives, after completing their mission, have to report to the judge and the judge has to enforce their decision. It must be stressed here that the mediators – when they decide on separation – have to give only one revocable divorce, so that time may be given to the spouses to reflect on their situation before final separation can take place.[16]

Abduh's view on the judicial process of divorce found acceptance among the reformers in some Muslim countries who thought that improvement in this area was badly needed because the unlimited power of the husband to repudiate his wife was grossly abused, hence making the lives of many Muslim women unbearable. His view was, therefore, incorporated into their legal systems and helped them to introduce such reform. Tunisia, for example, was one of a few Muslim countries which decided to introduce legal reform based on Abduh's view on judicial divorce. The Tunisian reformers argued that, 'In the case of discord between spouses, the Quran orders the appointment of arbitrators – yet what more obvious case of discord between spouses is there than a pronouncement of repudiation by the husband? And who is then better qualified to undertake the necessary function of arbitration than the official tribunals? On this ground, therefore, the right of a husband to repudiate his wife extra-judiciously was abolished.'[17] Thus, all divorce actions were prohibited, henceforth, from taking place outside the domain of the court.

The introduction of such reform has heralded two things. Firstly, it has empowered the court with an unrestricted power to compensate the wife for any injury endured as a result of the divorce; secondly, it ensures that both spouses are treated on an equal basis in this regard.[18] It is interesting to mention that Abduh's view regarding arbitration is shared not only by legalists (as we said earlier) but also by other scholars. For example, Muhammed Ali in his comment on Chapter 4, verse 35 says, 'This verse lays down the procedure to be adopted when a case for divorce arises. It is not for the husband to put away his wife; it is the business of the judge to decide the case. Nor should divorce cases be made too public. The judge is required to appoint two arbiters, one belonging to the wife's family and the other to the husband's. These two arbiters will find out the facts, but their objective must be to effect a reconciliation between the parties. If all hopes of reconciliation fail, a divorce is allowed, but the final decision for divorce rests with the judge who is legally entitled to pronounce it. Cases were decided in accordance with the directions contained in this verse in the early days of Islam.'[19]

Terms for Divorce

The Quran also deals with divorce issues in another verse which states: 'Divorce may be pronounced twice, and then a woman must be retained in honour or allowed to go with kindness. It is unlawful for husbands to take from them anything they have given them, unless both fear that they may not be able to keep within the bounds set by Allah; in which case it shall be no offence for either of them if the wife ransoms herself.'[20] In this verse, God explains that divorce may be pronounced twice, during which period reconciliation can take place; hence it is a revocable type of divorce, since the couple can still resume their marital life if they wish to do so. However, a third pronouncement would lead to irrevocable divorce, after which the spouses cannot re-marry, unless the woman marries another person first and that person also divorces her. In this case, she is allowed to re-marry her former husband if she desires to do so: 'If a man divorces his wife, he cannot re-marry her until she has wedded another man and been divorced by him; in which case it shall be no offence for either of them to return to the other, if they think that they can keep within the limits set by Allah. Such are the bounds of Allah. He makes them plain to men of understanding.'[21] This was done in order to deter a man from divorcing his wife without good reason.[22]

Timing of Pronouncement

Divorce, if it has to take place, must be pronounced when the wife is in a state of purity (*tuhr*), otherwise it is regarded as invalid.[23] The reason for not allowing the husband to divorce his wife during the state of impurity is that the husband is physically separated from her and this might induce him to press ahead with the separation. While if she is in a state of purity, he is physically close to her and in this case he might be persuaded to reconsider his decision. Anyway, if divorce takes place, the wife has to observe *idda* or the waiting period. This lasts for three months, during which time sexual intercourse is not allowed between the spouses. By the end of this waiting period, the separation becomes *final* and legally effective.[24] The reason for making the waiting period obligatory is to ensure the achievement of the following: first, to give the spouses more time to reconsider their attitudes and resolve their differences; second, to determine whether or not the wife is pregnant, for if she is expecting a child there is always a good chance that the spouses might be willing to effect a reconciliation.

Responsibility to the Ex-spouse

When separation becomes a reality, both spouses are encouraged to recognise and respect each other's rights. In particular, the Quran exhorts the man to be considerate and kind to his former wife.[25] Also, he is enjoined to act with due care and not allow her to be thrown out of her house. He must ensure that she may stay, if she wishes, with respect and dignity.[26] Moreover, he should properly maintain her and give her sufficient support.[27] Here, it must be noted that there are differences of opinion among scholars regarding the maintenance of divorced women. Some recommend that a divorcee is entitled to sustenance, which includes both the dowry as well as a financial allowance, whilst others insist that the payment of her maintenance should only continue for the period of *idda*, which is not more than three menstrual cycles. Our view in this case, however, is that the verse (Chapter 2, verse 241) contains general guidelines which give no indication of any specific amount of maintenance, or indeed any length of time that is needed to sustain the divorcee. It has left the door open to meet the financial circumstances of both spouses in the light of their social conditions. In the light of the above and taking into consideration the recommendation made by the Quran (that the interests of the divorcee ought to be protected and safeguarded), we are of the opinion that the payment of the maintenance should be extended beyond the three months waiting period. The payment has to continue until the divorcee remarries or be in a position where she is no longer in need of his financial help. This is certainly in line with the spirit of social justice in the Quran.

DIVORCE UNDER ISLAMIC LAW

Under Islamic Law, the marriage contract may be dissolved in three ways: first, the death of one of the spouses; second, by act of the husband or the wife or both of them; third, through Judicial process or a decree of court.[28]

The dissolution of the marriage contract by the husband is called *Talaq* (divorce), which is usually translated as repudiation. It can be done unilaterally by the husband without his having to produce any reason.[29] This form of divorce or *talaq* has been classified (by the jurists) into three main types:

(1) *Talaq al-Ahsan*. This is the most approved form of repudiation. In this kind of *Talaq* the husband has to pronounce one single divorce (not two or three) during *tuhr* or the period of purity of the wife. Then he must abstain from having physical contact with her (i.e. sexual intercourse) during the waiting period. This form of repudiation is revocable. For the husband can, before the end of the *idda*, revoke the divorce and resume the conjugal relationship. It must be noted here that the approval of the wife is

essential in this context. The husband cannot force her back, even if he regrets divorcing her. She must first give her consent before the couple can resume their matrimonial relations. In order for him to signal his intention to retain her, he may express this desire either explicitly or implicitly. The former is the preferred one, and is usually done by pronouncing the revocation of the repudiation. If, during the waiting period, one of the spouses dies, the other can still inherit the estate. If the husband allows the waiting period to elapse without reclaiming his wife, the repudiation becomes irrevocable or absolute (*bayan*). The wife henceforth becomes free to contract a new marriage, be it with her former husband or with someone else.[30]

(2) *Talaq al-Hasan*. This is a less approved form of divorce. Here the husband repudiates his wife three successive times over a period of three months, once each month during the period of *tuhr*. As with *Ahsan talaq*, the husband can revoke his divorce after the first or second repudiation, but after the third repudiation the divorce becomes absolute (*bayan*). The only difference is that the wife cannot re-marry her former husband until she has first married someone else and then dissolved that marriage.[31] The reason for adding this condition is to prevent a hasty repudiation on the part of the husband.[32]

(3) *Talaq al-Bid'ah* (innovative). This is the least approved method of divorce in the Muslim world but, unfortunately, it is the most widely used. It is highly condemned by women and civilised men and regarded as sinful. Nonetheless, it is considered legally effective once it is pronounced. This form of divorce 'is effected by three repudiations, which may be pronounced at any time (not merely in clean periods) and without definite intervals'.[33] It is an irrevocable form of *talaq* and the husband can only re-marry his ex-wife after she has contracted a new marriage with a second man and dissolved that marriage (after proper consummation).[34] *Bid'ah* divorce lacks any Quranic support. Also, it was strongly denounced by the Prophet, who is reported to have reacted angrily when he heard that somebody had divorced his wife by the triple pronouncement of *talaq* in a single sitting and said 'How would you play with the book of Allah while I am alive and amidst you?'[35] He then ordered the man to take back his wife. Nonetheless, this innovative divorce acquired legitimacy under the reign of the second Caliph Umar, who decided to make it legal in an attempt to prevent any careless use of the formula. However, his efforts in this context proved to no avail as his decree eventually produced counterproductive results. Since then it has remained lawful and legally effective among Sunnis (the Shia do not recognise this type of divorce), and men

have continued to make use of it to their own advantage. We are therefore strongly in favour of banning it outright. It is a bizarre and odd practice; most importantly, it is very degrading to the dignity of Muslim women. Also, it allows men to indulge their whims, completely unfettered, with no obligation to honour their family responsibilities.

It is interesting to notice that the great jurist, Ibn Taymiyyah, was against it. He stated that the erratic use of such a practice (triple pronouncement on a single occasion) was invalid and had no impact on the statutory position of a marriage. His aim was to protect women, as he thought that they were victimised by such a ruling (Umar's validation of *Bid'ah* divorce). It is a shame that his position has been forgotten and disregarded in contemporary Muslim societies.[36]

The dissolution of marriage by the wife takes two forms: (1) *Talaq al-Tawfid*, or delegated divorce. In this form of divorce the husband, at the time of marriage, agrees to delegate to his wife the power of pronouncing the *talaq*, thus allowing her to dissolve the marriage contract. It must be stressed here that once the husband consents to give his wife the right to divorce him, he is no longer in a position to reclaim it. *Tawfid* divorce is indeed a powerful weapon in the hands of the wife, since she can easily use it if the conditions in the marriage contract are violated by the husband. But I wonder how many Muslim women can afford to take advantage of it, considering the social menace and terror surrounding them in Muslim societies.[37] (2) *Khula*, also called ransom by some jurists.[38] Here, the wife initiates the divorce, but the husband has to agree[39] to free her in return for re-payment of part or all of the dowry or *mahr*.[40] A woman seeking *khula*, however, may lose her right to maintenance during the waiting period.[41] Women's right to *khula* was acknowledged and respected during the early Islamic era; they were very often allowed to exercise it without fear or intimidation. For a woman to request *khula* she does not have to quote any specific reason; the fact that she is unhappy with her husband would be enough to grant her separation under *khula*.

This point is clearly illustrated by the following incident that took place during the Prophet's lifetime: 'The wife of Thabit bin Qais came to the Prophet and said, "O Allah's Messenger! I do not blame Thabit for defects in his character or his religion, but I, being a Muslim, dislike to behave in an un-Islamic manner (if I remain with him)". On that Allah's Messenger said (to her), "will you give back the garden which your husband has given you (as *mahr*)?" She said, "yes". Then the Prophet said to Thabit, "O Thabit! Accept your garden, and divorce her once".'[42] *Khula* is hardly ever practised these days. Indeed, the majority of Muslim women are not aware of its existence, let alone allowed to make use of it. And even if they know of it, alas, who dare to seek *khula* even if the husband looks like a monster or beast? It would certainly cause God's throne to tremble.

Divorce through mutual consent is usually called *Mubara'ah*. This form of divorce centres around an agreement between spouses to release each other from the marital link[42] with no exchange or payment on either side.

The final method of dissolving the marriage contract is through a judicial process, at the instigation of either the wife or husband. This can be obtained in the case of (a) *Lian* and (b) annulment.[44] *Lian* is a divorce by oath and it occurs when the husband accuses his wife of committing adultery without evidence.[45] The court, after studying the case and hearing particular oaths[46] from both spouses, would issue a decree allowing the marriage to be dissolved. This form of separation is irrevocable and the partners cannot re-marry each other again.[47] Annulment: the annulment (or *faskh*) of the marriage takes place when the wife lodges a complaint against her husband on the basis of the following: impotence, failure to fulfil the marital obligations, maltreatment, insanity and any other causes which might justify the annulment of the marriage. After investigating the complaint carefully, the judge would pass a court decree freeing the woman from the marital bond.[48]

CONCLUSION

Although the Quranic legislation on divorce aims at protecting women and allowing them to free themselves from the marital bond if it becomes necessary, in today's situation, there is a huge gap between the Divine principles and the actual practice. For example, most women are hardly allowed to exercise their right to divorce because of the tremendous social and mental pressures to which they are subjected. To break these barriers, they would need enormous courage, and few of them have this capacity. Therefore, divorce has become an exclusive right of men. And this right has been grossly abused. Indeed, in most cases, it has been deliberately used to suppress, control and humiliate women. And it must be stressed that, despite some improvements in recent years in some countries, the overall situation still remains far from perfect. Hence, urgent reform on divorce proceedings in general is sorely needed, and particular attention should be directed to the investigation of the motives for divorce on the part of men.

8 Women and Political Action

From the Islamic viewpoint, human actions are all regarded as duties, which in turn can be divided into *fard'ayn* (individual duty) and *fard kifaya* (collective duty). Duties in general (whether *fard'ayn* or *fard kifaya*) are closely linked with human ability, that is, they are obligatory on people who are able to fulfil them for 'Allah does not charge a soul with more than it can bear'.[1] It follows that political actions are also viewed as duties and hence can be classified as *fard 'ayn* (such as *Bay'a* or oath of allegiance and *Shura* or consultation) and *fard kifaya* (such as Jihad, public offices and enjoining good and forbidding evil). The obligatory nature of any actions (*Wajib*), including the political ones, is based on the concept of vicegerency or human representation of God on earth (*Khilafa*), which includes both men and women[2] and entails personal as well as corporate responsibility to fulfil God's commands on earth. Both then, as equal partners, share the onus or duty of running the political affairs of their society for they 'are friends (*awliya'*) to each other ... enjoin what is just and forbid what is evil'.[3] And, as we know, all the works of the Judiciary, Executive and Legislative powers are there to enjoin good and forbid evil. The Muslim woman, therefore, like her counterpart – the man – has a broad political responsibility and an important role to play in public life, a role that was put at the service of the nascent Islamic community in Medina and for a while thereafter in the early period of Islam. For women, especially during the Prophet's time, were very active socially and politically. They were allowed and even encouraged to participate in the process of building up the Medinan society and they proved to be up to the task.

EARLY POLITICAL ACTIVITIES OF MUSLIM WOMEN

Muslim women started their political activities the moment they embraced Islam.[4] They defended the new religion against fierce opposition from both their own families and society at large; they endured abuse and ill treatment[5] and when pressure mounted against them they decided to leave home, seeking refuge with their fellow Muslims rather than abandon their belief and faith.[6] All these actions are regarded as political activities in contemporary terms since they include a challenge to the old political system, a protest against unjustified abuse and torture, and a rejection of suppression and denial of freedom of belief and expression. With the establishment of the Islamic state, the role of women in the political affairs of the new society gained momentum. They became part of the nation and effective members of the community, fully involved in public affairs. For instance, right from the beginning, women, like men, gave support and allegiance to the political system which was set up under the leadership of Muhammad. This was done through the so-called *bay'a*.[7]

But what is *bay'a*? *Bay'a* in Islam is an important political institution by which the nation or the Umma grants or ensures legitimacy for the political system. It includes a pledge by the nation to be loyal to the system and its leader as long as this leader upholds Islamic principles.[8] Hence it is a covenant (*mithaq*) entered into by three parties: the leader (who is to be given the pledge or recognition; the nation or Umma (which is to give its allegiance and loyalty);[9] and the Sharia (which is to be respected and upheld by both the leader as well as the nation). *Bay'a* moreover, is divided into *bay'a 'ayniya*, related to the political commitment (*iltizam*) to the system, and is compulsory on every Muslim man and woman, and *bay'a kayfiyya* related to particular duties and is obligatory on a particular group of men and women. During Muhammad's leadership, allegiance and loyalty[10] were given to him by both men and women without any difference in content or responsibility.[11] For he took a pledge from women, as from men, to support the state and obey him in enjoining good and forbidding evil (*bay'a 'ayniya*). Also, he received *bay'a kayfiyya* from some prominent women; among them was Nusaiba bint Kab, who gave her word to participate in Jihad and indeed she did take part in many battles alongside men. This illustrates her determination to fulfil the *bay'a* despite the fact that it was *bay'a kayfiyya*; for this kind of *bay'a* is mandatory on those men and women with special talents. As she thought herself to be one of them, she decided to go ahead and fulfil it. This indicates that women (like men) are under an obligation to realise their individual capabilites to the full, and thus to take up the specific duties related to these capabilites, whether these duties be individual or collective.[12]

In addition to *bay'a*, women also participated in *Shura* (mutual consultation) which is one of the foundations of the Islamic political system. The practice of Shura is obligatory on both the leader as well as the Umma. The Quran says, 'Take counsel with them in the conduct of affairs; and when you are resolved, put your trust in Allah'.[13] We also have the verse which praises those 'who obey their Lord, attend to their prayers and conduct their affairs by mutual consent'.[14] In these verses, it is clear that the ruler is required to consult with the ruled, while the Umma is bound in its turn to offer counsel to the ruler.

Shura or mutual consultation is a tool by which the nation can achieve the objectives of the *Sharia*. Therefore, it is the responsibility of the nation to uphold it, protect it and under no circumstances allow it to be abandoned. The exercise of Shura can take place at different levels; hence the commitment to practise it by the individual members of the community varies according to the subject under consultation on the one hand, and on individual ability, on the other. For example, regarding legislative matters concerning *Sharia*, consultation is required with scholars or the *Ulama*; regarding technical issues, consultation is mandatory with experts in these fields; for general issues concerning the whole nation, some form of consultation with every member of the community would be ideal. This could take the shape of a referendum or general elections. Within this context, women can take part in consultation at various levels depending on the subject matter and on individual capability. For instance, they can participate in consultation at the legislative level, experts' level, or at the general public level as ordinary members of the community.

Women were consulted at all levels during the period of the Prophet's rule and that of his companions. They used to seek their advice (*mashwara*) before most important decisions were made. For example, the Prophet used to receive delegations of women presenting their cases to him. Among them was Asma bint Yazid al-Ansari, who was an outspoken woman. She used to speak and argue on behalf of her fellow Muslim women, and the Prophet used to encourage her and expressed his admiration for her strong personality.[15] His wives, especially Umm Salama and Aisha, never hesitated to ask searching questions and speak their minds when they felt it necessary; and the Prophet admired this questioning attitude. In fact, on one occasion, he had to rely on the advice (*mashwara*) of one of his wives, Umm Salama, to solve a problem that bewildered the Muslims at a crucial time of the Islamic history. Umm Salama with her wisdom, prudence and good judgement helped the Prophet to solve the predicament, thus avoiding a situation that could have divided the community and weakened Muhammad's mission.[16] Aisha, renowned for her wit and intelligence, was trained by the Prophet to question, discuss, argue and correct, to the extent that he recommended that the Muslims should learn from her knowledge and wisdom, especially in religious matters: take half of your religion from Aisha he said. By the time the Prophet passed away she had already become a great scholar and attained the position of a religious judge.[17] She was accepted as a religious authority during the caliphate of Abu Bakr, Umar and Uthman. Very often they used to consult her and seek her advice if they were faced with difficult issues. If they disagreed with her, the judgement she recommended turned out to be the correct one and then it was gladly accepted. Also, she gave a verdict in favour of one companion against another and at a certain stage she criticised and corrected them.[18] Her eloquence and qualities were described in these words: 'I have heard the speeches of the Khulafa, Abu Bakr, Umar, Usman, and Ali. But the words which came from the mouth of Aisha had a quality and excellence which is not in the words of anyone else.'[19] Hafsa, the daughter of the second caliph Umar, and one of the wives of the Prophet, was also active in public affairs. Her insight and guidance were very often sought by the companions. For example, on one occasion her father had to consult her before he could take a decision regarding the time limit for a husband to be away from his wife. (Also, based on his consultation with other women, he either amended or cancelled decisions, which he thought would run contrary to the interests of women.) Hafsa, moreover, expressed her concern about the political situation following the assassination of her father. While he was on his death bed she urged her brother Abdullah to discuss the issue with her father and ensure a smooth and peaceful transition of power. Also, she played a crucial role in persuading her brother, who was unwilling to get involved in the conflict that erupted between Ali and Muawiyah, to attend the arbitration which was set up to discuss the conflict and solve the problem peacefully and amicably.[20]

Contrary to the traditional image of women being secluded and suppressed, women in early Islam participated in armed conflict either by organising food and water and taking care of the wounded or through playing a crucial part in the actual fighting when it was needed. Among the many examples of women who took active part in the battles was Safiyya, an aunt of the Prophet, who defended a fortress in Medina at the time of the Battle of the Trench. She noticed an intruder who had penetrated the defences of the fortress; she managed to manoeuvre and kill him before he was able to do any harm to the women and children.[21] Women also reached positions of high responsibility as was the case with al-Shafa' who was appointed by the second Caliph Umar as a market inspector in Medina. Their involvement in politics, furthermore, manifested itself by the fact that they were alert and actively opposed to any rulers who they thought were deviating from implementing Islamic principles and maintaining a just society. Two examples can be cited in this context. First, there is the case of the woman who publicly opposed Umar for passing a law restricting the dowries of women. He was forced, after admitting his mistake to repeal his decision.

The second case was that of Aisha who genuinely believed that it was within her right to oppose the fourth caliph Ali and fight him for failing to find the murderers of Uthman. She led an army which included prominent companions such as Talha and Zubayr and fought a battle that was to be named the Battle of the Camel, because of the camel she was riding. Women's influence in public affairs reached its climax when their action to protect or give immunity from punishment were sanctioned by the Prophet. He approved and accepted all the *Ijara* (protection) cases licenced by women, this being a clear indication by the Prophet and the early community, of the ability and capacity of women to judge wisely and act responsibly even in matters of great concern to the stability and security of the Islamic state. There are many examples in which women accorded protection or asylum (*Ijara*) and the Prophet gladly supported them. It has been reported that the Prophet never opposed or rejected any *Ijara* extended to enemies by women.

It must be stressed that the high level of political (as well as social) activities performed by women in early Islam could not have been achieved without the realisation of three important and interrelated factors: first, the recognition of the political ability or competence of women. As we noticed above, women were regarded as fully-fledged citizens capable of participating in all political activities (including *bay'a*, *shura*, granting asylums, taking part in Jihad and holding prominent positions) and indeed they were allowed to do so; second, this recognition or acknowledgement gained momentum when women became politically conscious or aware of their responsibilities in society. An awareness which Muhammad undertook to raise and promote among all women. This was accomplished through instructing women to gain knowledge and education and encouraging them to attend public gatherings (especially Eid celebrations, which often took place in mosques) even when they were menstruating this being an illustration that although women were at certain times relieved from the obligations of their daily worshipping, this did not lead to an automatic reduction in their duty to participate in annual public meetings. On the contrary, they were urged to attend Eid festivals and the congregational Jumah (i.e. Friday) prayers, which were regarded as general political meetings during which important issues concerning the whole nation were discussed and debated.[22] This provided the minimum level of political (as well as social) awareness needed for the majority of them, especially those whose domestic responsibilities prevented them from attending congregational prayers such as Friday prayers. To achieve maximum benefit for them, the Prophet, moreover, used to give them advice and guidance, especially when he learnt that they could not hear him properly during one of his Eid sermons.[23]

The Prophet actively supported those women with special abilities and a higher level of awareness and whose circumstances allowed them to attend the regular congregational prayers. In fact, he instructed men (their husbands or relatives) not to prevent them from doing so even if they wanted to attend the dawn and night prayers,[24] during which time the Quran used to be recited, explained and interpreted. Such sessions formed the basis for their religious education as well as their social and political awareness. In addition, in order to satisfy their intellectual needs, the Prophet designated a special day for this group of women in which he used to teach them the principles of Islam and other related issues.[25] This raised the self awareness of Muslim women and increased their understanding of their responsibility in society,[26] leading, consequently, to greater public participation; and third, the broad political participation of women which was conditioned by their abilities and their degree of self-awareness was practised in a favourable social setting that gave it its stimulus and momentum. This supportive environment was the result of determined efforts, by the Prophet, to eradicate any practices and habits that would hinder or resist the progress towards wider political engagement of women in society. Hence, he pushed ahead the process of social change and ensured that the community would accept and regard women's activity in the political sphere as an asset and a valuable contribution to a healthy society. This was fulfilled: firstly, through the Quranic injunctions and *Hadith* regulations, both of which encourage women to be energetic and creative, while at the same time, exhort men to help them fulfil their roles as active and equal members of the community; secondly, the example set by the Prophet in dealing with his family in particular and the companions (women) in general.[27] He constantly encouraged them to take part in all aspects of life: social, political, economic and religious. This support found its echo when women, especially the Ansari women, demonstrated their interest and eagerness to participate in all activities, thus, setting a role model for other women to follow.[28] In doing so, they pioneered the way for radical social change that allowed more space and greater mobility for women in society.[29]

THE RETREAT OF MUSLIM WOMEN FROM PUBLIC LIFE

Despite the clear-cut Quranic and *Hadith* instructions encouraging women to play an effective role in public life (alongside their private one), the general tendency, among Muslims, has been one which opposes women's involvement in politics. Most scholars prefer an interpretation that enjoins women to stay at home and not to 'interfere' in public life. They argue that women are incapable of handling public affairs; therefore, it is better for them to perform the work they are good at – that is, to be mothers and wives only. According to them, women never participated in the politics of the Muslims throughout their history. And, it is argued that despite the fact that Islam gave women rights equal to those of men, Islam deems it necessary that women should stay at home and concentrate on their domestic affairs, in the interest both of women themselves and of society as a whole.[30] But one might object, what about the different social, political and economic activities played by women during the Prophet's time? The scholars then respond by insisting that those were mere individual cases which cannot be cited to legitimise the participation of women in political affairs. Anyone who thinks to the contrary is mistaken, they say, and does not comprehend history. As for Aisha who played a prominent role in politics, they argue that although she fought a famous battle, in the end she regretted her act (for she should not have left her home and taken part in that battle) and asked for forgiveness. Consequently, it cannot be claimed that her act is a proof for the participation of Muslim women in politics, for it was an individual act which proved to be a complete failure.[31]

It is important to stress that those who oppose women's involvement in politics differ among themselves regarding the level or degree of women's exercise of power. For example, while some are prepared to tolerate the idea that women can have limited access to politics (such as the right to vote and nominate persons for certain public offices), others deny them any political rights. However, they all agree that women cannot be allowed to hold ministerial positions or become prime minister or president of a state. They base their prohibition on the following:

(1) *Quran*: they maintain that Chapter 4, verse 34 of the Quran which reads thus: 'Men have authority over women because Allah has made the one superior to the other, and because they spend their wealth to maintain them', has virtually closed the door to women's advancement to higher positions. For them, this verse has sanctioned men's authority over women and made the domain of politics or power an exclusively male preserve. This is because men have strong leadership characteristics which entitle them to rule over women who tend to be weak and more emotional.[32] According to them, the verse is clear in entrusting men (not women) with the *Qiwama* or guardianship. It follows that since men are the caretakers (*Qawwamun*) of women, it is not possible for them to hold positions of authority which would allow them to exercise power over men. Moreover, they argue that even if they have to accept the view which states that this verse deals specifically with family affairs and

cannot be generalised to include male–female relations in public life, the proof (*hujja*) still stands: women cannot rule over men. For if they are unqualified to manage their family undertakings, by the same token, they are unfit to handle public matters.

However, we are of the strong opinion that this verse (4: 34) deals exclusively with family affairs and has nothing to do with the relationships between men and women in public life. This is because the verse is mentioned solely within the context of married life,[33] in which one party – the husband – is charged with the responsibility of being the head and caretaker of the family – bearing in mind that relieving the wife from such a responsibility is by no means an indication of her inability to do the job properly; on the contrary, she can easily replace him if he is absent (for whatever reason) or unfit to fulfil his duty. Therefore, it is not right to generalise the ruling of this verse (which handles only marital matters) to encompass the relationships between men and women in society, so as to deny women the opportunity to hold public offices.[34]

(2) *Hadith*: Two *Hadiths* are of particular importance in this issue. The Prophet is reported to have said 'O women! Give alms, as I have seen that the majority of the dwellers of Hell-fire were you (women). They asked, why is it so, O Allah's Messenger? He replied, you curse frequently and are ungrateful to your husbands. I have not seen anyone more deficient in intelligence and religion than you. A cautious, sensible man could be led astray by some of you. The women asked, O Allah's Messenger! what is deficient in our intelligence and religion? He said, is not the evidence of two women equal to the witness of one man? They replied in the affirmative. He said, this is the deficiency in her intelligence. Isn't it true that a woman can neither pray nor fast during her menses? The women replied in the affirmative. He said, this is the deficiency in her religion'.[35] This *Hadith* is used, by the opponents of women's rights in politics, to prove their point in saying that women cannot be trusted with handling public matters. They stress that the above *Hadith* makes it clear that women cannot have power over men because they are spiritually as well as cognitively deficient. They thus associate deficiency with womanhood and insist that women, by nature, are less prepared (rationally and emotionally) than men to cope with the pressure of public life. Therefore, God, according to them, has relieved them from certain duties (such as attending Jumah prayers and participating in Jihad) which are compulsory for men.[36]

However, there are those who see the *Hadith* differently: some do not accept it and consider it as fabricated or at best a weak *Hadith*, which ought to be abandoned because weak *Hadiths* usually do not carry any legal effects;[37] others acknowledge the *Hadith* as authentic, but stress that it has been grossly misinterpreted. They argue that the deficiency mentioned in the *Hadith* does not refer to natural but rather specific deficiency. In other words, there are two forms of deficiencies: (a) natural or innate deficiency (*naqs fitri*), a form of natural defect which hampers the human intellect at various levels, the extreme one being madness. This does not include women categorically because they are regarded (from the Quranic viewpoint) as accountable and responsible human beings capable of fulfilling their duties; (b) specific deficiency (*naqs naw'i*) of two types: (i) casual defect (*aradi*), which can temporarily upset the natural disposition of a person, especially during menstruation and pregnancy. This form of frailty does not weaken or impair women's natural abilities; (ii) incidental defect of long-term effects which results usually from living in special conditions (such as confinement to four walls, constant engagement in pregnancy and childbirth, etc.) that are not conducive to contacts and interactions with outside world. This, in time, lessens women's social, political and economic awareness of their surroundings and reduces them to their private circle of ladies, with devastating consequences on their potential for playing an active role in public life. It must be stressed, however, that this form of deficiency can be remedied by altering the circumstances that lead to its existence.[38]

As for the link made in the *Hadith* between women's intellectual deficiency and their testimony in law, we might point out that the connection occurs only in one case, namely, the evidence which requires the testimony of one man and two women. This testimony is mentioned in the Quran in Chapter 2, verse 282, which deals solely with financial matters. And this is the only testimony in which the issue of gender is a dominant factor; in other testimonies the Quran stipulates justice rather than gender. Therefore, it is not right to use this verse in order to accuse women of being intellectually deficient. For it is no more than a guiding verse aiming at promoting justice when dealing with complicated financial issues. In other words, the verse is meant to give advice that if, under certain circumstances, men are not available to testify, the alternative is to accept the testimony of two women (who could be ordinary members of the public, having little or no experience with financial matters, or who could be undergoing temporary disturbances resulting from menstruation or postnatal conditions) as being equal to that of man; the aim here being to ensure that precautionary measures are in place when dealing with an area where women are less likely to be experts. Overall, the deficiency referred to in the *Hadith*, therefore, is not natural but rather contingent or casual and does not necessarily contradict the fact that there are women who possess high qualities and enjoy special capacities in comparison with ordinary men and women. Indeed, in some cases there are those who are wiser, well-advised, and more intelligent than men.[39]

The second *Hadith* which is reported in Bukhari and reads as thus: Abu Bakra said 'when Allah's Messenger was informed that the Persians had crowned the daughter of Kisra (Khosrau) as their ruler, he said, such people as ruled by a lady will never be successful.'[40] This *Hadith* has been widely cited to block any attempts to give women the opportunity to wield power in society. The opponents argue that the Prophet in this *Hadith* advises Muslims not to follow in the footsteps of the Persians who appointed a woman as their leader and consequently led them to a disastrous end. For them, the *Hadith* contains a clear-cut warning (for Muslims) to be vigilant and not to allow women to overstep the line and enter into politics; otherwise, their fate would be the same as that of Persia before Islam: defeat and humiliation.[41] However, one has to disagree with this view for two reasons: first, the *Hadith* deals mainly with a specific case, namely, the situation of Persia at the time of the Prophet.[42] Indeed, it is no more than a prophesy (*bishara*) in which the Prophet predicted the fate of the Persian empire. As such, it has no legal ruling and therefore it cannot be generalised to include all women at all times; second, if the *Hadith* is to be accepted as general, it would surely contradict the Quran, and this cannot happen. The Quran, in chapter 27, speaks highly of the Queen of Sheba, Bilqis, who ruled over her people with wisdom and insight and led them to success and prosperity 'I found a woman reigning over the people. She is possessed of every virtue and has a splendid throne'. The only fault found with her, was not her position and authority as a woman, but her false faith 'she and her subjects worship the sun instead of Allah'. Later, the wise woman met Solomon, admitted her sin (for not worshipping God) and, along with her people, accepted Islam: 'Lord', she said, 'I have wronged my own soul. Now I submit with Sulayman to Allah, Lord of the creation'.[43] From the above, we can deduce that the Hadith is not general, but rather specific and is related to the episode of the people of Persia.

(3) *The practical experience of the early community*: the opponents point out that there is no precedent in early Islam which indicates that women were appointed to high positions, despite the fact that there were ample opportunities for such appointments. Neither the Prophet nor any of his companions invited women to take part in the administration of the state. Moreover, women themselves, and although there were many who

excelled men in their abilities, did not show any interest in holding public office. In response, one can mention the example of the second Caliph Umar, who appointed a woman (al-Shafa') as superintendent in a market in Medina. This position was, at the time, more of a political than a business office, as the market was not only a centre for trading but also a focal point for political activities. Also, the fact that few women were at the top of the administration does not reflect badly on the abilities of women to run public offices. Moreover, one has to bear in mind the nature of the social setting prevailing at the time, in which pre-Islamic customs were still competing and resisting any changes brought about by Islam.[44] So, although the social environment was favourable (due to the changes brought about by Islam) and allowed women greater mobility in society; yet it was still less willing and less amenable to the idea of entrusting women with governmental positions. However, social practices (*'Adat*) should not be allowed to take precedence over Divine instructions. Most importantly, they should not be used as a pretext to continue to neglect or even (in some cases) abandon the Islamic principles, which oblige women to have their shares in public life and be active and effective in society. For social customs are subject to change; they change with time and place, while Divine principles are meant for all times and all places. As such, the emphasis should be on the Divine tenets not social customs.[45]

(4) *The Consensus (ijma)*: there are those who stress that there is an agreement among scholars on the so-called 'unsuitability' of women to hold public office. However, invoking the issue of consensus is no more than a fallacy since there is hardly any unity among them on this subject. For example, the position of Judge is regarded by some to be suitable for men only; Abu Hanifa, however, disagrees and allows a woman to be appointed as Judge and gives her the right to deal with all matters except those under the penal code. Ibn Jarir al-Tabari, on the other hand, qualifies a woman for the post of judge without any restrictions. This renders the whole issue of the existing consensus among scholars suspicious and, in fact, a mere sham. Moreover, it is essential to bear in mind whether the *ijma* (on a particular question, and, in this case, the issue of women) takes into consideration the overall interest of the community. For if it runs counter to the social interest, then there is no use in accepting it in the first place.

(5) *Maslaha* (welfare): the opponents argue that permitting women to occupy public positions would be detrimental to both society as well as family. According to them, top jobs require courage, wisdom and strength,

and women, in general, lack these characteristics; they are feeble and can be easily misled. As such, they cannot be trusted with executive roles, especially leadership roles. For instance, a president or a ruler in an Islamic state needs to perform important and not merely ceremonial duties such as: conducting war, signing peace treaties, defending the country, delivering sermons, and leading people in prayers – all of which women cannot cope with, because of their fragilities and emotional vulnerabilities. Furthermore, they state that woman's advancement to executive power goes against her social function: that is to be a good wife and mother. They argue that if she is to assume an executive role – which is a full-time commitment – this would inevitably force her to neglect her household duties, with devastating consequences on the stability of the family in society. They point out that even if there are some women who can handle both roles, they are, in reality, exceptions; therefore, it is unwise to set up and accept rules on rare cases. It must be stressed, however, that those who think that female leadership would damage state-interest base their view on the assumption that women are, by nature, incapable of coping with public responsibilities. But this is not the case as we explained earlier; women, like men, are qualified to run state affairs. Also, the opponents view public positions, especially state leadership as a one-person responsibility, thus neglecting the *shura* principle, which makes state affairs a collective responsibility. Moreover, they regard the state system as more or less similar to that of the Medinan or tribal system with limited scope and structure, hence, confining the Islamic concept of state within a particular historical context. In doing so, they contradict the universal vision of the Islamic state.

As for the welfare of the family, the assumption is that only those women whose domestic responsibilities permit them to engage in public duties should do so. Having said that, domestic responsibility should not be taken as pretext (by both men and women) to discourage or prevent women, especially able ones, from involvement in public activities. In other words, women should strike a balance between their domestic and public commitments and try and avoid a situation whereby one commitment overshadows the other. This means that, in essence, only a few women would be able to qualify in terms of this criterion. Hence, the standard of judgement should be based on the few not on the majority as the opponents claim. This is because prominent jobs are usually based on ability and merit rather than on gender.[46]

(6) *Cut the pretexts* (*Sadd al-Dhārā'i*): the opponents stress that leadership positions require public display and constant contacts with people.

This would inevitably facilitate mingling between the two sexes; an issue which is clearly prohibited in Islam. According to them, the Quran explicitly orders women to stay at home and avoid any public exposure; therefore, it is not appropriate for them to take on public duties, because this would expose them to all forms of public immorality. In response, we can say that this view is certainly out of context with both the Quran as well as the practical Sunnah of the Prophet. For instance, the Quran in Chapter 33, verse 32[47] ordered (solely) the Prophet's wives to stay at home and not to display any public appearance, because they were regarded as the mothers of the believers; other women were not included. For they used to take part in public worship, seek knowledge and education, participate in Jihad, enjoy wider social interactions, and attend vocational training. So, the verse deals with a specific case, namely, the status of the Prophet's wives, and therefore, it is not right to generalise it to include other Muslim women; in doing so, they reject the practical Sunnah of the Prophet, and this cannot be right. It must be made clear, moreover, that of all social interactions only *Khulwa* (seclusion), promiscuity, lustfulness, and extravagance or excessiveness are prohibited in Islam. Other societal activities, which are needed for the conduct of normal and respectable social life are allowed and encouraged. So, to use *fitna* (temptation) as an excuse in order to change a religious ruling is indeed unjustifiable. For women, especially nowadays, cannot perform their duties without meeting men. Also, it must be remembered that God, who is the legislator, knows better what the state of his creatures is in terms of their piety or corruption.

When Islam encouraged women to take part in public life, it did so by laying down certain rules of conduct, so as to curb any tendency towards *fitna* or corruption. It did not show any inclination to restrict or prevent women from mixing with men under the pretext of *fitna*. This is despite the fact that many unpleasant incidents occurred, especially during the Prophet's time, as a result of the wide social contacts that prevailed between the two sexes. Nevertheless, those incidents were regarded as exceptions, and they did not disturb or stop the normal course of social life.[48] To portray women as a source of temptation and corruption conveys a message which is based on lack of confidence in women themselves. Most importantly, it shows a complete disregard for their dignity as independent and rational human beings, and that is certainly against the very essence of Islam.

To conclude, it is clear that Islam has granted women full political rights. Contrary to the view which opposes women's involvement in politics, there is no evidence in the scripture which suggests that women are not entitled to play an active role in politics. Also, an examination of the early history of Islam at the time of the Prophet, shows that women were not kept aloof from politics, rather they were encouraged to be at the forefront of the political affairs of their society. As for leadership positions, it is true that they require particular abilities, but it is equally true that there are women who have talents and skills and are capable – like men – of handling public offices, including ministerial and presidency offices. As such, there are no grounds or justification for those who oppose female leadership. In fact, their argument neither has a theological rationale nor is it in line with current reality.

9 Conclusion

It has become apparent from this study that contrary to the general misconceptions, women in Islam – at least theoretically speaking – are entitled to full rights as citizens. These rights were put into practice during the Prophet's time and in the period of the early Caliphate, during which women enjoyed the privilege of fulfilling their private as well as their public duties. Early Muslim society never embraced the concept of social division of labour between the two sexes. It entertained no such ideas as the differentiation between public and private roles, as far as women were concerned, nor the subordination, as is the case today, of public life to the private one. Indeed, both roles were equally valued, and women were expected to enjoy and excel in them. Whilst performing their public duties, women were not encouraged to be secluded, confined or constrained, nor were they forced to form a world of their own, separate, invisible and totally cut off from the so-called men's world. Both sexes mixed and worked together within the rules of conduct laid down by Islam in order to build up their society. In the process, they encouraged and helped each other irrespective of their sex or status. In their relations with one another, they transcended all evil thought currently prevailing in most Muslim societies: there were no ill-feelings, sexual temptation or lust. This atmosphere of peace, harmony and piety uplifted their spirits and transformed them into creative and resourceful human beings respecting and respected by others. In other words, it was a healthy society, primarily because women were highly revered and honoured, for they realised that the spiritual, material and intellectual progress of a society is closely linked with the position of its women, and that no society which enslaves its women would ever prosper.

This bright picture began to be clouded with the decline of the first caliphate. Like other aspects of Muslim lives, the position of women started to deteriorate. Slowly but surely their rights faded away: firstly, they were discouraged from taking part in public life; secondly, they were ordered to withdraw and hide behind four walls. This was done by separating the private from the public role and subordinating the latter to the former. Hence, and in time, women became passive, yielding and publicly less visible, with little involvement in public matters. It was left entirely to men, who were only too happy to take over, to decide their own destiny. For centuries women were forced to accept humiliation and exploitation.

To ensure they were kept under their whips, the ultra-conservatives used many misogynistic interpretations of Islam. Under the false name of Islam they virtually stripped women of every right: no to education, no to instigating divorce, no to travelling alone, no to leadership positions, no to work outside the house, and so on.

This form of repression was bound to create, eventually, rebellion, especially among the educated elite who had to rebel against the status quo and lead the liberation movement. But the secular feminists in their quest for change decided to break away with the tradition and fully embrace Western ideals. So convinced are they by the superiority of Western values that they see no way for the liberation of Muslim women other than via the Western model, to the extent that they believe that to be Western is to be free and to be Muslim is to be a slave. Content that they have chosen the right path for salvation, they launched a crusade against anything to do with Islam. For example, they have bitterly attacked and ridiculed the very foundations of Islam; expounded views which are alien and contradictory to the spirit of the Islamic faith; made a mockery of the Islamic principles; showed no sensitivity towards their own culture; formed a class of their own very much out of touch with the needs of ordinary women; tolerated no criticisms or dissenting views; presented women's case in a sensational way and used language often transcending all bounds of decency; demonstrated no sympathy or understanding towards the views of ordinary Muslim women. Indeed, they have displayed self-righteous and self-conceited attitudes, viewing themselves as superior to 'ordinary' Muslim women.

This approach is doomed to failure; indeed it has already backfired, since it alienates sections of Muslim women who want change but not at the expense of losing their religious identity (some have argued that the latter are a minority, but it should be stressed that they are a strong minority, mostly educated or living in the West, who have come to appreciate their own Islamic heritage). These women have become less receptive to the secular feminists' views and ideas and even questioned the validity of a model which did not, after all, provide adequate answers to their problems. Moreover, they have alienated a group of men whose support and co-operation is essential to achieve the expected change in society. There is no doubt that many misogynistic notions are prevalent in Muslim societies, but these can only be eradicated by advocating authentic Islam. It must be stressed, however, that propagating true Islam does not mean fundamentalist Islam; for the latter has nothing to offer other than a distorted image of Islam. Rather, the emphasis must be on the Islam of Aisha, Khadija, Fatima, and Umm Salama: all well-known Muslim figures and excellent role models for inspiration.

I am sure there is a great deal to learn from the West, but first and foremost any attempt to improve the position of Muslim women must come from within: 'God does not change the condition of a people until they change it for themselves' said Muhammad. It is only through the authentic Islamic way that Muslim women will achieve freedom and self-respect, and will be able to demonstrate the beauty of their religion and dispel the misconceptions surrounding the true position of Islam regarding women.

Notes

THE LEGAL STATUS OF WOMEN IN ISLAM

1. For more details of women's status in the pre-Islamic period see, Muhammad Yusuf Abd, *Qadaya al-Mar'a Fi Surat An-Nisa*, Dar-al-Dawah, Kuwait, 1985, pp. 15–28.
2. Divorce was common among all nations of antiquity. Generally speaking, the power of divorce was vested in the hands of the husband. The wife was very often denied the right to ask for divorce 'under the old rabbinical law a husband could divorce his wife for any cause which made her distasteful to him. Among the Athenians as well as the early Romans, the husband's right to repudiate the wife was as unrestricted as among the Israelites. In later times, among the Hebrews, the Shammaites to some extent modified the custom of divorce by imposing certain restrictions on its exercise, but the school of Hillel upheld the law in its primitive strictness. At the time of the prophet's preachings, the Hillelite doctrines were chiefly in force among the Jewish tribes of Arabia, and repudiations by the husbands were as common among them as among the pagan Arabs'. See Syed Razi Wasti, *Syed Ameer Ali on Islamic History and Culture*, People's Publishing House, Lahore, 1968, p. 225.
3. On this point see A.M. Al-Aqqad, *al-Mar'a Fi al-Quran al-Kareem*, Dar al-Hilal, Cairo, 1959, p. 87.
4. See S.A.A. Mawdudi, *Purdah and the Status of Woman in Islam*, Islamic Publications Ltd, Lahore, Pakistan, 1976, p. 2.
5. Let us cite some examples: in India 'subjection was a cardinal principle. Day and night must women be held by their protectors in a state of dependence. The rule of inheritance was agnatic, that is descent traced through males to the exclusion of females'. In Hindu scriptures a good wife is 'a woman whose mind, speech and body are kept in subjection, acquires high renown in this world, and, in the next, the same abode with her husband'. 'Athenian women were always minors, subject to some male – to their father, to their brother, or to some of their male kin ... she was obliged to submit to the wishes of her parents, and receive from them her husband and her lord, even though he was a stranger to her'. 'In Roman law a woman was even in historic times completely dependent. If married she and her property passed into the power of her husband ... the wife was the purchased property of her husband, and like a slave acquired only for his benefit. A woman could not exercise any civil or public office ... could not be a witness, surety, tutor, or curator; she could not adopt or be adopted, or make will or contract'. See J. Badawi, *The Status of Women in Islam*, Gassim, Saudi Arabia, 1991, pp. 6–7. Also, Scandinavian women were 'under perpetual tutelage, regardless of their being married or otherwise. No woman was to marry without first getting the consent of her tutor, otherwise he could use his powers and make use of her property during her lifetime if he wished

100

so'. In China 'Unmarried women were members of their natal families, but on marriage a woman moved to the family of her husband and was afterwards subject to the authority of her husband's parents and seniors. Any property brought by the bride, apart from such items as personal ornaments, was transferred to the ownership of her husband's family'. 'Marriage was arranged by formal agreement between the heads of the family concerned, after negotiation usually conducted through a go-between according to the generally accepted forms'. See Said Abduallah al-Hatimy, *Women in Islam: A Comparative Study*, Islamic Publications Ltd, Lahore, Pakistan, 1993, pp. 6–8. In the Mosaic Law 'the wife was betrothed: To betroth a wife meant simply to acquire possession of her by payment of the purchase money; the betrothed is a girl for whom the purchase money has been paid'. The consent of the girl for marriage was invalid 'the girl's consent is unnecessary and the need for it is nowhere suggested in the Law'. 'The woman being a man's property, his right to divorce her follows as a matter of course. The right to divorce was held only by man; and 'divorce was a privilage of the husband only'. According to the early church 'woman was represented as the door of hell, as the mother of all human ills. She should be ashamed at the very thought that she is a woman. She should live in continual penance on account of the curses she has brought upon the world. She should be ashamed of her address, for it is the memorial of her fall. She should be especially ashamed of her beauty, for it is the most potent instrument of the devil'. 'Do you know that you are each an Eve? The sentence of God on this sex of yours lives in this age: the guilt must of necessity live too. You are the devil's gateway: you are the unsealer of that forbidden tree; you are the first deserters of the Divine Law; you are she who persuades him whom the devil was not valiant enough to attack. You destroyed so easily God's image, man. On account of your desert – that is death – even the Son of God had to die'. See Badawi, *The Status of Women in Islam*, op. cit., pp. 9–11.

6. For a comprehensive discussion of the social, political, economic and religious background of Arabia before Islam see W. Montgomery Watt, *Muhammad at Mecca*, Oxford University Press, Oxford, 979, pp. 1–23. Also, see Hammuda Abd al-Ati, *The Family Structure in Islam*, American Trust Publications, 1977, pp. 5–11.

7. The Quran forbade this practice. Chapter 4, verse 19 says: 'O believers, it is unlawful for you to inherit the women of your deceased kinsmen against their will, or to bar them from re-marrying, in order that you may force them to give up a part of what you have given them'.

8. The Quran prevented such practice. 4: 19 says: 'you shall not marry the women who were married to your fathers. That was an evil practice, indecent and abominable'. This verse was revealed when a woman came to the Prophet and informed him that her husband (Abu Qays) had passed away and therefore his son (Qays) had asked her to marry him. The Prophet's response was to recite this verse, thus banning such a custom. See Ibn Kathir, *Tafsir*, Dar al-Qalam, Beirut, Vol. 1, 1986, p. 370. Moreover, other types of women were also prohibited. 4: 23 reads thus: 'Forbidden to you are your mothers, your daughters, your sisters, your paternal and maternal aunts, the daughters of your brothers and sisters, your foster-mothers, your foster-sisters, the

mothers of your wives, your stepdaughters who are in your charge, born of the wives with whom you have lain; but it is no offence for you (to marry them) if you have not consummated your marriage with their mothers. (Forbidden to you also) are the wives of your own begotten sons and to take in marriage two sisters at one and the same time unless this had happened in the past. Allah is Forgiving and Merciful'. Also, 4: 24 '(Forbidden to you also) are married women, except those whom you own. Such is the decree of Allah. All women other than these are lawful to you, provided you seek them with your wealth in modest conduct, not in fornication. Give them their dowry for the enjoyment you have had of them as a duty; but it shall be no offence for you to make any other agreement among yourselves after you have fulfilled your duty. Allah is Knowing, Wise'. It is essential to mention that the Arabs before Islam did not allow the marriage of a man to the wife of his adopted son (or adopted daughter). Islam, on the contrary, approved it on the grounds that there is no blood relationship between the adopted son and the adopter which could hinder such a marriage. Islam maintains that adoption does not make the adopter the natural father of the adopted son. The Quran says, 'Name your adopted sons after their fathers; that is more just in the sight of Allah. If you do not know their fathers, regard them as your brothers in the faith and as your cousins. Your (unintentional) mistake shall be forgiven, but not your deliberate errors. Allah is Forgiving and Merciful' (33: 6). Also 'And (remember) when you (Muhammad) said to the man (Zayd, Muhammad's adopted son) whom Allah and yourself have favoured: Keep your wife and have fear of Allah. You sought to hide in your heart what Allah was to reveal. You were afraid of men, although it would have been more right to fear Allah. And when Zayd divorced his wife, We gave her to you in marriage, so that it should not be difficult for true believers to wed the wives of their adopted sons if they divorced them. Allah's will needs to be done' (33: 36). This verse was revealed when Zayd, the adopted son of the Prophet divorced his wife Zainab. Later, God decided for the Prophet to marry her. As the Arabs were not accustomed to this kind of marriage, they opposed it. Hence this verse was sent to clarify the issue (meaning, from the Islamic viewpoint, the adopted son is not a real son and therefore should not be treated as such). See Al-Tabari, *Jami al-Bayan an Ta'wil al-Quran*, al-Halabi and Sons, Egypt, Second Edition, Vol. 22, 1954, pp. 12–15.

9. See Sona Khan, *Understanding of Islam and Its Notions*, Paper submitted to the Euro-Islam conference, Stockholm, June 1995, p. 6. Also, see V.R. and L. Bevan Jones, *Women in Islam*, Lucknow Publishing House, Lucknow, 1941, p. 27.

10. Shah Abdul Qayyum, 'Women in West Asia – A Case Study of Egypt', *Islam and the Modern Age*, Vol. IV, No. 3, 1973, p. 54. Also, see V.R. and L. Bevan Jones, *Women in Islam*, op. cit., p. 14.

11. *The Quran*, 16: 56.

12. *The Quran*, 81: 1–10.

13. Malik Ram Baveja, *Women in Islam*, Advent Books, New York, 1981, pp. 1–2.

14. Said Abdullah Seif al-Hatimy, *Women in Islam: A Comparative Study*, op. cit., p. 18.

15. R. Levy, *The Social Structure of Islam*, Cambridge University Press, Cambridge, 1965, pp. 91–2.

16. John L. Esposito, 'The Changing Role of Muslim Women', *Islam and the Modern Age*, Vol. IV, No. 3, 1973, p. 54.

17. The various types of sexual union which prevailed in Arabia before Islam is related by the Muslim traditionist al-Bukhari: 'Ibn Shihab said, Urwah Ibn al-Zubair informed him that Aisha, the wife of the Prophet (God bless and preserve him) informed him that marriage in the *Jahiliyah* was of four types: (1) one was marriage of people as it is today, where a man betroths his ward or his daughter to another man, and the latter assigns a dowry (bridewealth) to her and then marries her; (2) another type was where a man said to his wife when she was purified from her menses, send to N. and ask to have intercourse with him; her husband then stays away from her and does not touch her at all until it is clear that she is pregnant from that (other) man with whom she sought intercourse. When it is clear that she is pregnant, her husband has intercourse with her if he wants. He acts thus simply from the desire for a child. This type of marriage was known as *Nikah al-Istibda*, the marriage of seeking intercourse; (3) another type was where a group (*raht*) of less than ten men used to visit the same woman and all of them to have intercourse with her. If she became pregnant and bore a child, when some nights had passed after the birth she could send for them, and not a man of them might refuse. When they had come together in her presence, she would say to them, You (pl.) know the result of your acts. I have borne a child and he is your (sing.) child, N., naming whoever she will by his name; her child is attached to him and the man may not refuse; (4) the fourth type is where many men frequent a woman, and she does not keep herself from any who comes to her. These women are the *baghaya* (prostitutes). They used to set up at their door banners forming a sign. Whoever wanted them went in to them. If one of them conceived and bore a child, they gathered together to her and summoned the physiognomists to designate as father the man whom the child resembled most. Then the child remained attached to him and was called his son, no objection to this course being possible. When Muhammad (God bless and preserve him) came preaching the truth, he destroyed all the types of marriage of the *Jahiliyah* except that which people practise today'. Translation from W. Watt, *Muhammad at Medina*, Oxford University Press, Oxford, 1988, pp. 378–9. There were also other forms of marriages: (1) called *Mut'a* marriage (marriage of pleasure, or temporary marriage): Bukhari mentions it as such 'if a man and a woman agree to live together, their partnership lasts three nights and if they want to extend it, they extend it, and if they decide to part, they part'. Translation from Fatima Mernissi, *Beyond the Veil*, al-Saqi Books, London, 1985, p. 77. It must be stressed that *Mut'a* marriage was practised in early Islam, but it was prohibited later on according to Sunni sources. However, today among Shia Muslims, *Mut'a* marriage is still in force; (2) *al-Shighar*, a form of marriage in which a man could marry another man's daughter or sister. In return he would give in marriage his daughter or sister to him. During the marriage exchange, no dowry (*mahr*) would be offered to the bridegrooms. This type of marriage was prohibited under Islamic law. See Reuben Levy, *An Introduction to the Sociology of Islam*, Williams and Norgat Limited, London, Vol. 1, 1931, p. 150.

18. Cited in Fatima Mernissi, *Beyond the Veil*, op. cit., p. 67.

19. Tafsir al-Tabari, Vol. 4, p. 233.

20. See Reuben Levy, *The Sociology of Islam*, op. cit., p. 144.

21. The Verse reads thus: 'if you fear that you cannot treat orphans with fairness, then you may marry such women as seem good to you; two, three, or four of them. But if you fear that you cannot do justice, marry one only or those you possess. This will make it easier for you to avoid injustice'. When this verse was revealed there were many who had more than four wives. For example, Ghaylan ibn Salama had ten; Naufal ibn Muawiyah had five. The Prophet subsequently asked them to keep up to four, if they wished, and release the rest. See *Tafsir Ibn Kathir*, Vol. 1, p. 356.

22. The Quran stopped this custom. 24: 33 says 'You shall not force your slave-girls into prostitution in order that you may make money, if they wish to preserve their chastity. If any one compels them then surely after such compulsion, Allah will be Forgiving, Merciful'.

23. Although normally divorce was exclusively in the hands of men, there were exceptions to this rule: in one case, a woman could stipulate in her marriage contract that she would reserve the right to divorce her husband if she wished to; in another one, a woman would not marry unless her husband agreed to delegate to her full control over their own affairs. So, if she felt, at some stage of their lives, that she was no longer in love with him she could easily divorce him. Asghar Ali Engineer, *The Rights of Women in Islam*, C. Hurst and Company, London, 1992, p. 27.

24. It has been mentioned that a man from the family of Abu Talib in a moment of anger said to his wife 'Thy matter is in thy hands (I divorce you)'. The wife replied: 'By God. l was in your hands for twenty years; I guarded these years and gave you the best company. I did not waste a single moment and fulfilled all my duties'. He admired what she said and so made up with her. See Ibid., p. 27.

25. Ibid., p. 26.

26. In *Jahiliya*, there were many forms of divorce. Here are a few examples of them: *Khula*, a form of divorce in which a woman (through her father or guardian) could release herself from the marital tie after paying back the husband her dowry (*mahr*); *Ila*, a kind of divorce in which the husband would make an oath that he would leave his wife and have nothing to do with her; *Zihar*, meaning 'back', widely practised in Arabia before Islam. In this kind of divorce a man would say to his wife that she was like his mother's back. Consequently, she would become unlawful for him to touch just like his real mother. The divorced woman thereafter would marry another person who had previously agreed to do so with her former husband. See V.R. and L. Bevan Jones, *Women in Islam*, op. cit., pp. 27–9. It must be stressed that *Zihar* was among the worst kinds of divorce, to which Islam was categorically opposed. The Quran says 'Allah has never put two hearts within one man's body. He does not regard the wives whom you divorce as your mothers, nor your adopted sons as your own sons. These are mere words which you utter with your mouths; but Allah declares the truth and guides to the right path' (33: 1). Another form of divorce which prevailed in Arabia was called *al-adl* which meant prohibiting divorced woman from having a second chance of getting married. A man

who married a woman but found that he did not like her, would divorce her after forcing her to agree that she would not re-marry without his permission. Hence if somebody asked to marry her, he would act like a dictator: if he so wished he would give his permission, otherwise he would oppose and reject the whole process. See *Tafsir ibn Kathir*, Vol. 1, pp. 368–9. The Quran opposed such practice: 'O ye who believe! It is not lawful for you to forcibly appropriate women as part of heritage, nor should you subject them to duress with a view to taking away from them part of what you have given away to them, unless they are guilty of open immorality, and live with them in an appropriate manner. If ye dislike them in any manner, may be you have disliked that in which God hath placed abundant good for you'. See Abdul Kalam Azad, *The Tarjuman al-Quran*, (edited and rendered into English by Syed Abdul Latif), Kazi Publications, Lahore, Vol. II, undated, p. 218.

27. Islam regulated the waiting time (*idda*) for women: A divorced woman has to wait for three months before she can re-marry, whilst a widow is required to wait four months and ten days before she is allowed to contract a new marriage. 2: 228 says, 'Divorced women must wait, keeping themselves from men, three menstrual courses. It is unlawful for them, if they believe in Allah and the Last Day, to hide what He has created in their wombs: in which case their husbands would do well to take them back, should they desire reconciliation'. Also 2: 234 says, 'And those of you who die and leave wives behind, such wives should keep in waiting for four months and ten days after their husband's death. When they have reached the end of their waiting period, it shall be no offence for you to let them do whatever they choose for themselves, provided that it is lawful. Allah is cognizant of what you do'.

28. See Asghar Ali Engineer, *The Rights of Women in Islam*, op. cit., p. 30.

29. Abdur Rahman Doi, *Women in Shariah*, Ta-Ha Publishers Ltd, London, 1989, p. 83.

30. Also, Reuben Levy in *Sociology of Islam*, p. 134 writes: 'It is to be doubted whether more than a very few (women) had any degree of personal independence to the extent of being able to choose husbands for themselves, or even to have the disposal of property of any value. The cases which are often quoted to prove that the status of women was a high one are generally of exceptional people, and have for that very reason been preserved'.

31. Barbara Freyer Stowasser, 'The Status of Women in Early Islam', in Freda Hussein (editor), *Muslim Women*, Croom Helm, London, 1983, pp. 14–15.

32. For example, Chapter 6 (The Cattle) verses 137 and 141: 'And thus their associate-gods have induced many polytheists to kill their children so that they may ruin them and confuse them in their faith. But had Allah pleased, they would not have done so. Therefore, leave them to their false inventions'. 'Lost are those that in their ignorance have wantonly slain their own children and made unlawful what Allah has given them, inventing falsehoods about Allah. They have gone astray and are not guided'. And Chapter 17 (The Night Journey) verse 31: 'You shall not kill your children for fear of want. We will provide for them and for you. To kill them is a great sin'.

33. Cited in S.A.A. Mawdudi, *Purdah and the Status of Woman in Islam*, op. cit., p. 154.

34. Cited in M. Abdul-Rauf, *The Islamic View of Women and the Family*, Robert Speller and Sons, New York, 1977, p. 21.
35. Cited in Ibid., p. 21.
36. M. al-Siba'i, *al-Mar'a Bayn al-Fiqh Wal-Qanun*, al-Maktab al-Islami, Beirut, Damascus, 1962, p. 26.
37. *The Quran*, 3: 194.
38. *The Quran*, 33: 32.
39. *The Quran*, 16: 95.
40. *The Quran*, 9: 71.
41. Also, Chapter 48 (Victory) verse 5 '(He has done this) so that He may also bring the believers, both men and women, into Gardens watered by running streams, there to abide forever; that He may forgive them their sins, which is in Allah's sight a great triumph, and that He may punish the hypocrites and the idolaters, men and women, who think evil thoughts concerning Allah. A turn of evil shall befall them, and Allah's wrath is on them. He has laid on them His curse and prepared for them the fire of Hell: an evil fate'. And Chapter 57 (Iron) verse 11: 'The day will surely come when you shall see the true believers, men and women, with their light shining before them and in their right hands, (and a voice saying to them): Rejoice this day. You shall enter Gardens watered by running streams in which you shall abide forever. That is the supreme triumph. On that day the hypocrites, both men and women, will say to the true believers: wait for us that we may borrow some of your light. But they will answer: Go back and seek some other light!'.
42. 5: 37 says 'As for the man or woman who is guilty of theft, cut off their hands to punish them for their crimes. That is the punishment enjoined by Allah. He is Mighty, Wise. But whoever repents and mends his ways after committing evil shall be pardoned by Allah. Allah is Forgiving, Merciful'.
43. 24: 1 Says 'The adulterer and the adulteress shall each be given a hundred lashes. Let no pity for them detain you from obedience to Allah, if you truly believe in Allah and the Last Day; and let their punishment be witnessed by a number of believers'.
44. 24: 6 says 'And those who accuse their wives and have no witnesses except themselves, let each of them testify by swearing four times by Allah that his charge is true, calling down in the fifth time upon himself the curse of Allah if he is lying. But they shall spare her the punishment if she swears four times by Allah that his charge is false and calls down Allah's wrath upon herself if it be true'.
45. L. al-Faruqi, 'Islam and Human Rights', *The Islamic Quarterly*, Vol. XXVII, No. 3, 1983, p. 27.
46. *The Quran*, 2: 36.
47. Also 7: 27 'Children of Adam! Let the devil not deceive you, as he deceived your parents out of Paradise. He stripped them of their garments to reveal to them their nakedness. He and his companions see you whence you cannot see them. We have made the devils supporters of the unbelievers'.
48. *The Quran*, 7: 19–24.
49. *The Quran*, 20: 120.

50. S.A.A. Mawdudi, *Purdah and the Status of Woman in Islam*, op. cit., pp. 154–5.

51. L. al-Faruqi, 'Islamic Traditions and the Feminist Movement: Confrontation or Cooperation?', *The Islamic Quarterly*, Vol. XXVII, No. 3, 1983, p. 136.

52. S. Mawdudi, *Purdah and the Status of Women in Islam*, op. cit., pp. 150–5.

53. Lea Zaitoun, *Questions and Answers About Women's Rights in Islam*, World Assembly of Muslim Youth, Saudi Arabia, No date stated, p. 26.

54. *The Quran*, 4: 31.

55. For example Surah 4 verse 2: 'Give women their dowry as a free gift; but if they choose to make over to you a part of it, you may regard it as lawfully yours'.

56. Anis Ahmad, *Women and Social Justice*, Institute of Policy Studies, Islamabad, Pakistan, 1991, pp. 80–1.

57. Jamal Badawi, 'Women in Islam' in Khurshid Ahmed, *Islam: Its Meaning and Message*, The Islamic Foundation, Leicester, 1980, pp. 137–8.

58. Also, Surah 2 verse 186 '… they (your wives) are an apparel to you, as you are an apparel to them'.

59. *The Quran*, 30: 20.

60. Abdur Rahman. Doi, *Women in Shariah*, op. cit., p. 6.

61. Said Abdullah al-Hatimy, *Women in Islam: A Comparative Study*, op. cit., p. 25.

62. Naila Minai, *Women in Islam: Tradition and Transition in the Middle East*, John Murray, London, 1981, p. 10.

63. Said Abdullah al-Hatimy, *Women in Islam*, op. cit., p. 25.

64. 'Those who die and leave women behind should bequeath to them a year's maintenance without causing them to leave their homes; but if they leave of their own accord, no blame shall be attached to you for any legitimate course they may deem fit to pursue. Allah is Mighty and Wise. Reasonable provision should also be made for divorced women. That is incumbent on righteous men'. *The Quran*, 2: 240.

65. Naila Minai, *Women in Islam*, op. cit., p. 10.

66. *The Quran*, 39: 9.

67. *The Quran*, 58: 9.

68. *The Quran*, 20: 113.

69. L. al-Faruqi 'Women in a Quranic Society' in H. Tesbah, M. Bahonar and L. al-Faruqi, *Status of Women in Islam*, Islamic Propagation Organisation, Tehran, 1985, pp. 64–5.

70. S. Saeed, *Islam: from Revelation to Realization*, National Hijra Council, Pakistan, 1986, pp. 64–5.

71. Cited in M. Abdul-Rauf, *The Islamic View of Women and Family*, op. cit., pp. 106–7.

72. Ibid., pp. 107–12.

73. All cited in Ibid., pp. 109–12.

74. *The Quran*, 4: 7.

75. Jamal A. Badawi, *The Status of Women in Islam*, op. cit., p. 24.

76. Chapter 58 verse 1 says: 'Allah has heard the words of her who pleaded with you concerning her husband and made her complaint to Allah. Allah has heard the arguments of both of you. He hears all and observes all.' Also, Surah 60

verse 10: 'Believers, when believing women seek refuge with you, test them. Allah best knows their faith. If you find them true believers do not return them to the infidels; they are not lawful to the infidels, nor are the infidels lawful to them. But hand back to the unbelievers what they have spent. Nor is it an offence for you to marry such women, provided you give them their dowries. Do not hold on to the ties of marriage with unbelieving women: demand what you have spent and let them ask for what they have spent. Such is the law which Allah lays down among you. Allah is Wise and All-knowing'. And again, Verse 12: 'O Prophet, if believing women come to you and pledge themselves to associate in worship nothing with Allah, to commit neither theft, nor adultery, nor child-murder, to utter no monstrous falsehoods (concerning the fatherhood of their children), and to disobey you in nothing just, accept their allegiance and implore Allah to forgive them. Allah is Forgiving and Merciful'.

77.   Here we refer to the incident that took place during the Caliphate of Umar ibn al-Khattab. On one occasion, when Umar was discussing public issues in the Mosque, a woman present at the gathering argued with him, corrected him and caused Umar to state that he was wrong and the woman was right.

78.   Nusaiba and Asma were two women among 75 members of the delegation which went to the Prophet asking his permission to migrate from Mecca to Medina. See al-Hatimy, *Women in Islam*, op. cit., p. 51.

79.   Zainab, the daughter of the Prophet, mediated between her father and Abul Aas bin ar-Rabi and succeeded in gaining the approval of the Prophet to give him refuge and protection. See Ibid., p. 52.

80.   Abdur Rahman Doi, *Women in Shariah*, op. cit., p. 7.

81.   Ibid., p. 7.

82.   Muhammad Abdul-Rauf, *The Islamic View of Women and Family*, op. cit., p. 29.

83.   Mohammad Mazheruddin Siddiqi, *Women in Islam*, Adam Publishers and Distributors, New Delhi, 1988, pp. 15–16.

84.   On the relationship between the Prophet and his daughters see Muhammad Ali Qutb, *Banat al-Nabi*, Dar al-Qalam, Beirut, no date mentioned.

85.   Muhammad Abdul-Rauf, *The Islamic View of Women and Family*, op. cit., p. 26.

86.   *The Quran*, 31: 13.

87.   *The Quran*, 17: 21.

88.   Also: 'Someone asked (the Prophet) to whom he should show kindness and he replied: Your mother. He asked who came next and he replied, Your mother. He asked again who came next and he again replied, Your mother. He asked who came next and he replied, Your father, then your relatives in order of relationship'. 'A man came to the Prophet ... and said Messenger of God, I desire to go on a military expedition and I have come to consult you. The prophet asked him if he had a mother and when he replied that he had, he said: Stay with her, for Paradise is at her feet'. Abdulwahid Hamid, *Islam the Natural Way*, Muslim Education and Literary Services, London, 1989, p. 81.

89.   Aliah Schleifer, *Motherhood in Islam*, The Islamic Academy, Cambridge, 1986, pp. 12–24.

90.   Abdulwahid Hamid, *Islam the Natural Way*, op. cit., p. 72.

91. Muhammad Abdul-Rauf, *The Islamic View of Women and the Family*, op. cit., p. 25.
92. *The Quran*, 2: 186.
93. Abdur Rahman Doi, *Women in Shariah*, op. cit., p. 7.
94. Also, 'Once a woman came to the Prophet with a complaint against her husband. He told her: there is no woman who removes something to replace it in its proper place, with a view to tidying her husband's house, but that Allah sets it down as a virtue for her. Nor is there a man who walks with his wife hand-in-hand, but that Allah sets it down as a virtue for him; and if he puts his arm round her shoulder in love, his virtue is increased tenfold'. Cited in, Ibid., p. 10.
95. Naila Minai, *Women in Islam*, op. cit., p. 18.
96. Ibid., p. 18.
97. Said Abdullah al-Hatimy, *Women in Islam*, op. cit., p. 54.
98. For more discussion on this issue, see Ibn Sa'd, *Kitab al-Tabaqat*, Dar Sadir, Beirut, 1980, Vol. 8.
99. See Syed Razi Wasti, Syed Ameer Ali on *Islamic History and Culture*, op. cit., p. 50.

ISLAM AND WOMEN'S EDUCATION

1. M.O. Adeleye, 'Islam and Education', *The Islamic Quarterly*, Vol. XXVII, No. 1, 1983, p. 140.
2. Cited in G.N. Saqib, *Modernization of Muslim Education in Egypt, Pakistan, and Turky: A Comparative Study*, Islamic Book Service, Lahore, Pakistan, 1983, p. 42.
3. M.O. Adeleye, 'Islam and Education', *The Islamic Quarterly*, op. cit., p. 141.
4. This *Hadith* is testified to by the Quran in the following: '(Abraham and Ishmael Prayed): Our Lord! And raise up in their midst a messenger from among them who shall recite unto them Thy revelations and shall instruct them in Scripture and in Wisdom and shall make them grow. Lo! Thou, only Thou, art the Mighty, Wise'. 'He it is Who hath sent among the unlettered ones a messenger of their own, to recite unto them His revelations and to make them grow, and to teach them the Scripture and Wisdom, though heretofore they were in error manifest'. 'Allah verily hath shown grace to the believers by sending unto them a messenger of their own who reciteth unto them His revelations, and causeth them to grow, and teacheth them the Scripture and Wisdom, though heretofore they were in error manifest'. All are Cited in M. Hamidullah, 'Educational System in the Time of the Prophet', *The Islamic Culture*, Vol. 13, No. 1, 1939, p. 52.
5. Ibid., p. 59.
6. Cited in K.S.R. Rao, *Muhammad: The Prophet of Islam*, Islamic Propagation Centre International, United Kingdom, 1985, p. 22.
7. Ibid., pp. 22–3.
8. *The Quran*, 96: 1.
9. Afzalur Rahman, *Muhammad: Blessing for Mankind*, The Muslim Schools Trust, London, 1997, pp. 233–4.

10.   *The Quran*, 58: 9.
11.   *The Quran*, 39: 9.
12.   *The Quran*, 20: 113.
13.   All cited in M.O. Adeleye, 'Islam and Education', *The Islamic Quarterly*, op. cit., p. 141.
14.   All cited in Afzalur Rahman, *Muhammad Blessing for Mankind*, op. cit., pp. 238–9.
15.   Cited in: R.L. Gulick, Gr, *Muhammad: The Educator*, Institute of Islamic Culture, Lahore, Pakistan, 1969, p. 45.
16.   A. Shalaby, *History of Muslim Education*, Dar al-Kashshaf, Beirut, 1954, p. 165.
17.   M.A. Anees and A.N. Athar, 'Studies on Islamic Education: An Interpretive Essay', *The Islamic Quarterly*, Vols XX, XXl and XXll, No. 4, 1978, p. 159.
18.   Cited in A. Shalaby, *History of Muslim Education*, op. cit., p. 164.
19.   Ibid., pp. 165–70.
20.   G.N. Saqib, *Modernization of Muslim Education in Egypt, Pakistan, and Turkey: A Comparative Study*, op. cit., pp. 70–1.
21.   M. Hamidullah, 'Educational System in the Time of the Prophet', *The Islamic Culture*, op. cit., p. 53.
22.   M.O. Adeleye, 'Islam and Education', *The Islamic Quarterly*, op. cit., p. 141.
23.   G.N. Saqib, *Modernization of Muslim Education in Egypt, Pakistan, and Turkey*, op. cit., p. 66.
24.   S.H. Nasr, 'Islamic Education and Science', in Y.Y. Haddad, B. Haines, and E. Findly, *The Islamic Impact*, Syracuse University Press, USA, 1984, pp. 48–9.
25.   For more details, see George Makdisi, *The Rise of Colleges: Institutions of Learning in Islam and the West*, Edinburgh University Press, Edinburgh, 1981.
26.   S.H. Nasr, 'Islamic Education and Science', in Y.Y. Haddad, B. Haines, and E. Findly, *The Islamic Impact*, op. cit., p. 49.
27.   Ibid., pp. 50–1.
28.   G.N. Saqib, *Modernization of Muslim Education in Egypt, Pakistan, and Turkey: A Comparative Study*, op. cit., pp. 68–71.
29.   S.A.A. Mawdudi, *Purdah and the Status of Woman in Islam*, op. cit., p. 152.
30.   Fida Hussain Malik, *Wives of the Prophet*, S.H. Muhammad Ashraf, Lahore, Pakistan, 1979, p. 47.
31.   In Islam the spiritual growth and development are fully opened to the female sex. Hence, once a woman struggles in the spiritual life she would be in a position to acquire access to all the possibilities of the Islamic tradition and to become, like man, the vicegerent of God on earth. See, Saadia Khawar Khan Chishti, 'Female Spirituality in Islam', in S.H. Nasr (editor), *Islamic Spirituality*, Vol. 1, Routledge and Kegan Paul, London, 1987, p. 203. The Quran, on many occasions, makes it clear that as far as moral and spiritual development are concerned, men and women are equal. Both have the same chance to develop their spiritual and moral potentialities. The Quran says: 'But the believer who does good works, whether men or women, shall enter Paradise. They shall not suffer the least injustice' (4: 122). Explaining, eloquently, the spiritual equality granted to men and women in this verse, Taqi al-Din al-Hasani states 'praise be to God, who

created the earth and the heavens ... and gathered together the believers, men and women, and established the sacred law .... And the people of happiness obeyed Him and did His work, from among the dutiful men and women .... And when He exhorted the creatures to be obedient, He did not single out the men, but spoke of the Muslims, men and women, and the believers of both sexes and those who observed the law, men and women, and the verses dealing with this are many and are not secret'. Cited in Saadia Khawar Khan Chishi, *'Female Spirituality in Islam'*, op. cit., p. 213. The Quran also informs us about the spiritual achievements of some women and the rewards they received, as a result, from God. In this connection the following verses illustrate the point: 'But to the faithful Allah has given as example Pharaoh's wife, who said: Lord, build me a house with you in Paradise and deliver me from Pharaoh and his misdeeds. Deliver me from a wicked nation. And Allah has given as example Mariam, Imran's daughter, who preserved her chastity and into whose womb We breathed of Our spirit; who put her trust in the words of her Lord and His scriptures and was truly devout' (66: 11–12). 'We revealed this to Musa's mother' (28: 5). 'And (remember) when the angels said to Mariam: Allah has chosen you. He has made you pure and exalted you above all women' (3: 40). In the *Hadith* literature this spiritual equality has also been stressed. The following *Hadith*, which refers to both men and women, beautifully puts it thus: 'He who approaches near to Me one span, I will approach to him one cubit: and he who approaches near to Me one cubit, I will approach near to him one fathom, and whoever approaches Me walking, I will come to him running, and he who meets Me with sins equivalent to the whole world, I will greet him with forgivness equal to it'. Cited in Saadia Khawar Khan Chishti, *'Female Spirituality in Islam'*, op. cit., p. 201. Moreover, mention has to be made to the fact that some of the most famous mystics in Islam such as Khadijah (the Prophet's first wife), Aisha (the Prophet's beloved wife), Fatima (the Prophet's favourite daughter), Zubaydah (the Queen of Baghdad), and Rabiah al-Adawiyyah (the Queen of saintly women) were all women. Ibn al-Arabi, the great sufi scholar, expresses the spiritual equality between men and women thus: 'There is no spiritual quality pertaining to men without women having access to it also'. 'Men and women have their part in all degrees (of sanctity) including that of the function of pole'. Translated from Michel Chodkiewicz, *Le Sceau des Saints* (The Seal of the Saints), Gallimard, Paris, 1986, p. 126.

32. Malik Ram Baveja, *Women in Islam*, op. cit., p. 7.
33. In teaching the Muslims, Muhammad used to address both men and women together. Even on issues which are considered intimate or private he used to instruct them jointly. Abu Hurayra is said to have reported the following: The Prophet had just finished his prayer with us, when he directly turned and asked us to keep sitting, and then asked: Is there amongst you any who would shut doors and draw curtains when he approaches his wife, but would later go out and tell everybody how he did so and so? All men present kept silent. Then the Prophet turned to the ladies and said: Does any one of you openly discuss her conjugal matters with other women? A young lady in the audience, when she heard this, knelt up on one knee and craned her neck so that the Prophet might see her and hear her speak. She said: Yes by God,

all men discuss these matters among themselves and so do all women too. The Prophet said: Do you know whom does one doing that compare to? Indeed it is like two satanic couples who meet on a high street and indulge their sexual desire in full view of the people'. Cited in Hasan Turabi, *Women in Islam and Muslim Society*, Milestones, London, 1991, pp. 22–3.

34.   P.S. Ali, *Status of Women in the Muslim World*, Aziz Publication, Lahore, Pakistan, 1975, p. 28.

35.   A.S. Tritton, *Materials on Muslim Education in the Middle Ages*, Luzac and Co., Ltd., London, 1957, p. 140.

36.   S.A.A. Mawdudi, *Purdah and the Status of Woman in Islam*, op. cit., p. 152.

37.   Mohammad Mazheruddin Siddiqi, *Women in Islam*, op. cit., p. 17.

38.   Fida Hussain Malik, *Wives of the Prophet*, op. cit., p. 47.

39.   For more information, see Muhammad Zubayr Siddiqi, *Hadith Literature* (edited and revised by Abdal Hakim Murad), especially the chapter entitled 'Women Scholars of Hadith', Islamic Texts Society, Cambridge, 1993.

40.   P.S. Ali, *Status of Women in the Muslim World*, op. cit., pp. 16–29.

41.   R. Levy, *The Social Structure of Islam*, op. cit., p. 133.

42.   M.E.T. Mogannam, *The Arab Women*, Tonbridge Printer Ltd, London, 1937, p. 22.

43.   A. Shalaby, *History of Muslim Education*, op. cit., p. 195.

44.   M.E.T. Mogannam, *The Arab Women*, op. cit., p. 25.

45.   B.F. Stowasser, 'The Status of Women in Early Islam', op. cit., p. 34

46.   A. Shalaby, *History of Muslim Education*, op. cit., pp. 198–9.

47.   M.E.T. Mogannam, *The Arab Women*, op. cit., pp. 24–5.

48.   Shah Abul Qayyum, 'Women in West Asia', op. cit., p. 58.

49.   See, for example, Chapter 58 of the Quran entitled 'The woman who is arguing', particularly verse 1 which states 'Allah has heard the words of her who pleaded with you concerning her husband and made her complaint to Allah. Allah has heard the arguments of both of you. He hears all and observes all'.

50.   L.L. al-Faruqi, 'Islamic Traditions and the Feminist Movement: Confrontation or Cooperation?', *The Islamic Quarterly*, op. cit., pp. 135–6.

51.   See, for example, Muhammad al-Gazali, *Qadaya al-Mar'a*, Dar al-Shuruq, Cairo, 1991, p. 164.

52.   M. Abdul-Rauf, *The Islamic View of Women and the Family*, op. cit., p. 68.

53.   Malik Ram Baveja, *Women in Islam*, op. cit., p. 15.

54.   She is reported to have said 'I would give fodder to his (her husband's) horse, draw the water, patch his water skin, knead the flour. I was not good at baking and preparing bread; but I had some sincere Ansar neighbour ladies who used to help me with the baking. I used to bring, on my head, fruit kernels from the land which the Prophet had given to al-Zubair. That land was at a distance of three farsakhs (about ten miles). One day I was on my way home with a load on my head when I met the Prophet with a number of the Ansar. The Prophet asked me to ride behind him on the camel, but I felt shy of joining the company of men. The Prophet realised that I was feeling shy and, therefore, continued his journey without me'. Cited in Turabi, *Women in Islam and Muslim Society*, op. cit., p. 19.

55.   M. Abdul-Rauf, *The Islamic View of Women and the Family*, op. cit., p. 69.

56. P.S. Ali, *Status of Women in the Muslim World*, op. cit., p. 30.

57. Charis Waddy, *Women in Muslim History*, Longman, London and New York, 1980, pp. 3–4.

58. M. Abdul-Rauf, *The Islamic View of Women and the Family*, op. cit., p. 69.

59. John L. Esposito, 'The Changing Role of Muslim Women', *Islam and the Modern Age*, Vol. VII, No. 1, 1976, pp. 29–32.

60. Ann Dearden, *Arab Women*, Minority Rights Group, No. 27, London, 1983, p. 45.

61. Ghazy Mujahid, 'Education of Girls in Saudi Arabia', *Muslim Education Quarterly*, Vol. 4, No. 3, 1987, p. 48.

62. Cited in J.S. Szyliowic, *Education and Modernization in the Middle East*, Cornell University Press, Ithaca and London, 1973, p. 58.

63. This line of thinking is still prevalent in most Muslim countries, where some stress that co-education for both boys and girls is detrimental to the interest of the girls in that it prevents them from concentrating on those fields which would prepare them to be good wives and mothers; contradicting, therefore, the Islamic injunctions which make no distinction between the various branches of knowledge women can choose concerning their education. This view is supported by the following statement which advocates separate education for boys and girls: 'The most vital defect of co-education, from the point of view of female nature and woman's special functions in society, is that it prevents the training of woman for motherhood. How can a common educational institution run alike for boys and girls make adequate provision for training a woman in those arts and branches of knowledge which are necessary for her future life as a mother? Education for motherhood is the crying need of the world today. Because the vast majority of girls become mothers in after-life [sic], every girl should be required to specialise for a definite time in those subjects which will make her a good mother. When the whole curriculum of girls is hopelessly congested with subjects on the line of boys which cost them their mental equilibrium and physical health, their essential function in life is allowed to pass off in ignorance'. Cited in Mohammad Siddiqi, op. cit., p. 123.

64. M.K. Al-Oteiby, *The Participation of Women in the Labour force of Saudi Arabia*, MA dissertation, North Texas State University, Denton, 1982, p. 7.

65. Cited in Jane I. Smith, 'The Experience of Muslim Women', in Y.Y. Haddad, B. Haines and E. Findly, *The Islamic Impact*, op. cit., p. 103.

66. M. Abdul-Rauf, *The Islamic View of Women and the Family*, op. cit., p. 134–5.

67. John L. Esposito, 'The Changing Role of Muslim Women', *Islam and the Modern Age*, op. cit., pp. 33–5.

68. Jane I. Smith, 'The Experience of Muslim Women', in Y.Y. Haddad, B. Haines and E. Findly, *The Islamic Impact*, op. cit., p. 102.

69. J. Minces, *The House of Obedience*, Zed Press, London, 1982, pp. 72–4. Also, *The World's Women: Trends and Statistics*, United Nations, New York, 1995.

70. N. al-Sanabary, 'Continuity and Change in Women's Education', in E.W. Fernea, *Women and the Family in the Middle East: New Voices of Change*, University of Texas, 1985, p. 109.

71. I know a man who has recently decided to send his twelve-year-old son to England to learn English culture and language. When I inquired about the

possibility of his fourteen-year-old daughter accompanying her brother, he promptly answered me 'What she needs is basic elementary education which will prepare her for family domestic responsibilities'. This kind of mentality runs across large sections of the Muslim population, both male and female: an educated woman (with a university degree) told me that all she was hoping for her two (teenaged) daughters was to secure good marriages for them. 'What about their education? Would you not be proud if they went to university?' I asked. 'What for?' she questioned. 'Whether they are educated or not, in the final analysis, they have to get married. So the sooner they go to their husband's homes, the better' she replied happily, and then continued 'You know, nowadays it is very difficult to bring up daughters. Therefore, marriage is the best thing for them; it is sitr (protection) for them'. Unfortunately, as long as we continue to have this crude mentality, the world of Islam will never recover from its present backwardness and see the light of freedom and progress.

72. Debbie J. Gerner, 'Roles in Transition: The Evolving Position of Women in Arab-Islamic Countries', in F. Hussain, *Muslim Women*, op. cit., pp. 77–8.

73. N. al-Sanabary, 'Continuity and Change in Women's Education', in E.W. Fernea, *Women and the Family in the Middle East*, op. cit., p. 108.

74. For more information about women in Saudi Arabia, particularly upper class Saudi women see Soraya Altorki, *Women in Saudi Arabia: Ideology and Behaviour among the Elite*, Columbia University Press, New York, 1986.

75. M. Rehemi, *A Survey of the Attitudes of Saudi Men and Women Toward Saudi Female Participation in Saudi Arabian Development*, PhD thesis, University of Colorado, 1983, pp. 47–8.

76. E. Abdul-Rahman Hallawani, *Working Women in Saudi Arabia: Problems and Solutions*, PhD dissertation, Claremont Graduate School, 1982, p. 43.

77. Debbie J. Gerner, 'Roles in Transition: The Evolving Position of Women in Arab-Islamic Countries', in F. Hussain, *Muslim Women*, op. cit., p. 79. Also, see *The World's Women: Trends and Statistics*, op. cit.

78. M. Rehemi, *A Survey of the Attitudes of Saudi Men and Women Toward Saudi Female Participation in Saudi Arabian Development*, op. cit., p. 48.

79. Ghazy Mujahid, 'Education for Girls in Saudi Arabia', *Muslim Education Quarterly*, op. cit., p. 54.

80. F. Allaghi and A. Almana, 'Survey of Research on Women in the Arab Gulf Region', in *Social Science Research and Women in the Arab World*, Frances Pinter, London and Dover, Unesco, Paris, 1984, pp. 23–4.

81. M. Rehemi, *A Survey of the Attitudes of Saudi Men and Women Toward Saudi Female Participation in Saudi Arabian Development*, op. cit., p. 49.

82. M.K. Al-Oteiby, *The Participation of Women in the Labor Force of Saudi Arabia*, op. cit., pp. 62–6.

83. Ghazy Mujahid, 'Education for Girls in Saudi Arabia', *Muslim Education Quarterly*, op. cit., p. 60.

84. M. Yamani, 'Some observations on women in Saudi Arabia', in M. Yamani (ed.), *Feminism and Islam: Legal and Literary Perspectives*, Ithaca Press, Reading, 1997, p. 270.

85. A. McDermott, 'Saudi Arabia', in Ann Dearden, *Arab Women*, op. cit., p. 9.

WOMEN AND MARRIAGE IN ISLAM

1. The Quran says: 'He created you from a single being, then from that being He created its mate' (39: 5). Also, 'that Allah created the sexes, the male and the female' (53: 33). 'Was he not a drop of ejected semen? Then he became a clot of blood; then Allah created and moulded him and made of him the pair of male and female' (75: 36).

2. Qamaruddin Khan, *Status of Women in Islam*, Islamic Book Foundation, Lahore/Washington, 1988, pp. 26–9.

3. There are many Quranic verses which urge Muslims to get married: 'It was He who created man from water and gave him kindred of blood and of marriage. Your Lord is All-Powerful' (25–54). 'We have sent forth other apostles before you and given them wives and children' (13: 38), 'Lord, give us joy in our wives and children and make us examples to those who fear you' (25: 72). Also, the Prophet in his sayings emphasised the importance of the practice of marriage. Here are a few examples: 'Marriage is my Sunna. He who does not act according to my Sunna does not belong to me'. 'A person who marries achieves half his religion, so let him fear God in the other half'. 'No building is built in Islam more beloved to God than marriage'. 'A Muslim man can acquire no benefit after Islam greater than a Muslim wife who makes him happy when he looks upon her, obeys him when he commands her, and protects him when he is away from her in herself and his property'. All cited in Sachiko Murata, *The Tao of Islam*, State University of New York Press, New York, 1992, pp. 171–2.

4. Celibacy in Islam is described as undesirable, although it is not prohibited. It is reported that once the Prophet heard some of his companions planning to fast everyday, to stay up all night to worship and to leave the company of their wives. The Prophet denounced such tendencies and declared: 'I myself fast some days and do not fast some other days. I sleep part of the night, and stay up (in worship) the other part of the night. And I enjoy women through marriage'. Cited in M. Abdul-Rauf, *The Islamic View of Women and Family*, op. cit., p. 43.

5. In this context the Prophet is reported to have said: 'A woman may be chosen for her wealth, or for her beauty, or for her nobility or for her religion. So choose a religious woman and hold fast to her'. Cited in M. Abdul-Rauf, *Marriage in Islam*, Exposition Press, New York, 1981, p. 25. Also, the Quran clearly commands marriage to the pious, even though they may be poor or slaves: 'Take in marriage those women among you who are single and those of your ... slaves who are honest. If they are poor, Allah will enrich them from His own abundance' (24: 32).

6. H. Abd al-Ati, *Islam in Focus*, American Trust Publications, Indiana, 1976, pp. 114–5.

7. Al-Ghazali describes it as such 'Know that marriage is one part of the way of religion, like eating food. For the way of religion has need of human life and subsistence, and life is impossible without food and drink. In the same way it needs the subsistence of the human species and its procreation, and this is not possible without marriage. Therefore, marriage is the cause of the origin of existence, while food is the cause of the subsistence of existence'. Cited in S. Murata, *The Tao of Islam*, op. cit., p. 172.

8. The disadvantages include the following: the risk that the marriage may prove to be a futile exercise. This would lead to the breakdown of the marital relationship, with devastating consequences on both sides. The situation would be more difficult if there are children involved. The breakdown of the family could have long-lasting effects on their livelihood. Another risk involves the restrictions which are imposed on the individual freedom of the married partners. This includes such issues as the adjustments which both have to make to meet the wishes, demands and attitudes of the other, and the burden (both financial and otherwise) which the partners have to bear in raising children and looking after the welfare of the family as a whole. See M. Abdul-Rauf, *Marriage in Islam*, op. cit., pp. 20–2.

9. Al-Ghazali eloquently explains this in the following statement. 'The ... merit of having children is that a person should have striven for that which is loved by God: that is, human existence and procreation. Whoever understands the wisdom of the created order will have no doubt that God loves this. For God has given His servant an earth worthy of cultivation. He has given him seed. He has turned over to him a pair of oxen and a plough. He has sent a deputy to encourage him to cultivate. If the servant has one iota of intelligence, he knows what God means by all this, even if He should not speak to him with his tongue. God created the womb. He created the organ of intercourse. He placed the seed of the children in the backs and bodies of men and women. He sent appetite as His deputy to men and women. No intelligent person will miss what God means by all this. If the person should waste the seed and send away the deputy through some stratagem, without doubt he will remain far from the road of what was meant by his original nature (*fitrat*). This is why the early Muslims and the companions considered it reprehensible to die while single. So much was this the case that when Muādh's two wives died in the plague and he himself caught the plague, he said, 'Give me a wife, that I may not die single'. Cited in S. Murata, *The Tao of Islam*, op. cit., p. 173.

10. This is based on the following famous *hadith*: 'When the son of Adam dies, nothing would be of more benefit to him except three things: a continuous charity (i.e. a trust), some useful knowledge he has left behind and a child who may pray for him'. M. Abdul-Rauf, op. cit., p. 15.

11. The Prophet said 'A child will carry its parents towards Paradise'. Also a child, on the Day of Judgement, would be told: 'Enter Paradise'. He will go to the door of paradise and say in an angry voice: 'I will not enter paradise without my Parents'. It will then be said to him: 'Admit his parents along with him in Paradise'. Quoted from al-Ghazali, *Ihya Ulum al-Din*, Book II, translated by Fazlu Ul-Karim, Sind Sahar Academy, Lahore, Pakistan, undated, p. 25.

12. The Quran says: 'You shall not draw near to adultery, for it is foul and its way is evil' (17: 32). Also, the Prophet said: 'There is no sin after shirk (associating others with God) more gross in the sight of God than a drop of semen which a man places in the womb which is not lawful for him'. Again, in this context, Abdullah ibn Musud (a companion of the Prophet) is reported to have said 'I asked the Messenger, may God bless him and grant him peace: Messenger of God, which is the biggest sin? He replied: to set up rivals with God by worshipping others though He alone has created you.

What next? I asked. To kill your child lest it should share your food. What next? I asked. To commit illegal sexual intercourse with the wife of your neighbour, he replied'. Both cited in H. Hamid, *Islam the Natural Way*, op. cit., p. 89.

13. Cited in S. Murata, *The Tao of Islam*, op. cit., p. 173.

14. Also, the second Caliph Umar is said to have remarked: 'Nothing better has been given to a man after faith than a virtuous wife. No wealth is compared as valuable to a man as a chaste wife'. Cited from al-Ghazali, *Ihya Ulum al-Din*, op. cit., p. 28.

15. Cited in M. Abdul-Rauf, *Marriage in Islam*, op. cit., p. 19.

16. Cited in Ibid., p. 20.

17. One of these rights is to treat them with respect and dignity. Listen to what the Quran has to say about wives: 'Treat them (wives) with kindness' (4: 19). As for mothers and motherhood, see the Quran (31: 13) and (17: 21). Also, the Prophet is reported to have said 'Shall I not tell you of the gravest of the major sins? It is to associate others with God and to disobey parents'. The gravity of the sin of making a mother unhappy and the rewards of gaining her satisfaction and blessing are beautifully illustrated by the following story: 'There was a young man at the time of the prophet, Alqamah by name. He devoted himself to worship. He became seriously ill and his wife (informed the Prophet). The Prophet summoned three of his trusted companions and told them: Go to Alqamah and let him recite the Shahadah. (They did what they were asked to do with him), but the words would not come from his tongue. They reported this to the Prophet, who then asked: Is either of his parents alive? and was told that his mother was. (The prophet asked her): tell me the truth .... How has your son Alqamah been? Messenger of God, she said, he performs much salat, fasts and gives a great deal in charity. And how are you (to him)? Messenger of God, I am angry with him. Why? O Messenger of God, he preferred his wife against me and disobeyed me. Thereupon the prophet said: The anger of Alqamah's mother has certainly prevented Alqamah's tongue from uttering the Shahadah. He then asked Alqamah's mother (to forgive him, declaring that) Alqamah will not benefit from his prayer, his fasting and his charity so long as you remain angry with him (so she forgave him). Thereafter Alqamah's tongue was released and he repeated the words of the Shahadah. That very day he passed away'. Both cited in A. Hamid, *Islam the Natural Way*, op. cit., p. 80.

18. It is essential to state that the concept of child marriage – a custom widely practised in some parts of the Muslim world – is not in its essence an Islamic rule; it is an old conventional practice.

19. From the Islamic point of view, 'piety and God fearing' are two essential elements in selecting a partner. It has been mentioned that 'a man asked advice of al-Hasan, the grandson of the Prophet, saying, "A number of men have asked for the hand of my daughter. To whom would you advise I should give her away?" al-Hasan replied: "Give her to the one who fears God most. If he loves her, he will treat her very well. And if he does not love her, he will not be bad to her, out of fear of God".' Cited in M. Abdul-Rauf, *Marriage in Islam*, op. cit. p. 26.

20. It is important to mention temporary or *Mut'a* marriage, currently practised among the Shia population (*Imamiyas*) of Iran. This kind of sexual union

was originated in Arabia before Islam. It was a form of short-lived alliance between a man and a woman who was chiefly looking for protection and support from her own tribe. As such she enjoyed a favourable position. For example, she continued to live among her own people and kept a close link with them, maintaining at the same time their support and protection. Also, the children who were born during such a union stayed among the woman's people and their descent was traced via their mother's lineage. This was the norm, irrespective of whether the father chose to stay permanently or otherwise among his wife's people.

Temporary marriage was practised in early Islam, but shortly afterwards it was banned by the Prophet (some say the prohibition was sanctioned by Umar, the second Caliph). Hence, the practice ceased to exist among the majority of Muslims except the Shia (*Imamiyas*), who have taken a totally different view regarding the ban: they have dismissed the prohibition as sheer fallacy and continued to practise it until the present time.

Mut'a is an Arabic word; it means enjoyment or pleasure. Hence, *mut'a* marriage is a union in which a woman agrees to cohabit with a man purely for sexual favours, for a specified period of time, in return for a fixed remuneration. This is done on the assumption that there would be no marriage (*nikah*) or divorce issues as is the case with permanent marriage. Also, the contract which establishes this kind of union does not call for mutual rights of inheritance between the two parties. After the termination of marriage, the waiting period (for women) is two menstrual cycles or 45 days (this is in contrast to the permanent marriage which requires a three-month waiting period). *Mut'a* marriage, in our view, is incompatible with the dignity of women as human beings. Because its purpose is purely sexual, it devalues and demeans women. In fact it is an insult to them, a form of religious licence for legal prostitution. Also, this kind of marriage is against the very basic concept of marriage in Islam: that is, to establish the marital relationship on a sound, solid and stable foundation. Therefore, we are of the view that this practice should be banned and outlawed. For an interesting account of the subject see S. Haeri, *Law of Desire: Temporary Marriage in Iran*, Tauris and Co. Ltd, London, 1989.

21. H. al-Ati, *Islam in Focus*, op. cit., pp. 116–7.
22. See H. al-Turabi, *Women in Islam and Muslim Society*, Op. cit., p. 16. Also, see Al-Bukhari, *Summarized Sahih al-Bukhari*, Maktabat Dar-Us-Salam, Saudi Arabia, 1994, p. 893.
23. The Prophet on many occasions stressed that a person wanting to marry a woman should have the opportunity to look at her before giving his final approval. Mughirah b. Shubah, a companion of the Prophet, is reported to have said 'I sought a woman in marriage. The Prophet asked if I had seen her. No, said I. He said "Then look at her, because it is more proper that love should be cemented between you".' Cited in M. Siddiqi, *Women in Islam*, op. cit., p. 49.
24. See Muhammad Sayyid Tantawi 'In the light of the Quran', in M. al-Ghazali, M. Tantawi, A. Hashim, *Women in Islam*, Dar al-Akhbar, Cairo, 1991, p. 63.
25. All cited in M. Siddiqi, *Women in Islam*, op. cit., p. 49.
26. *The Quran*, 2: 235.

27. See Ibn Sa'd, *Kitab al-Tabaqat*, Vol. 8, pp. 230–1.
28. See Ibn Sa'd, *Kitab al-Tabaqat*, Vol. 8, pp. 265–7. Also, L. Ahmed, *Women and Gender in Islam*, Yale University Press, New Haven and London, 1992, p. 76. Also see al-Asqlani, *al-Asaba*, Dar al-Kutub al-'Ilmiya, Beirut, 1995, Vol. 8, pp. 227–8.
29. A woman by the name of Khansa bint Khidham reported 'that her father gave her in marriage when she was a matron and she disliked that marriage. So she went to Allah's messenger and he declared that marriage invalid'. See Bukhari, *The Book of Marriage*, p. 895. In another tradition, ibn Umar says: 'Uthman b. Mazun died and left behind a young daughter. My uncle, Qudamah, gave her in marriage to me, without even consulting her. When the girl came to know of this, she hated this union and wished to marry Mughirah b Shuban. So she was allowed to marry Mughirah'. See Abdul Halim Abu Shaqqa, *The Liberation of Women at the Time of the Prophecy* (in Arabic), Dar al-Qalam, Kuwait, 1994, Vol. 5, p. 72.
30. There are many examples of Muslim women who made good use of this right so as to achieve some form of autonomy for themselves *vis-à-vis* their marriage partners. It must be stressed, however, that the ability to gain such control or autonomy was and still is conditional, in many cases, upon a variety of factors. These include: social and economic status, the awareness and knowledge of the Law, and the tenacity and resoluteness on the part of the woman concerned. Aisha bint Talha and Sukaina bint al-Hussein were two women of this kind. Aisha was Abu Bakr's granddaughter. She was famous for her knowledge, beauty and independence. She contracted three marriages during her lifetime and exercised a great deal of control over her married life. Sukaina, on the other hand, was the grand-daughter of the fourth Caliph Ali. She was celebrated for her beauty, wit and insight. A strong-willed woman, she married six times; in one marriage she herself took the initiative and ended the marital link, while in another she stipulated an unbendable term in her marriage contract. Among those terms were the right to have a monogamous relationship whilst she was still married to her husband and that he would not object to the way she was running her life.

    The experiences of Umm Salama and Umm Musa, two women representing medieval Islam, illustrate further good cases in point; they too exercised considerable authority over their married lives. Umm Salama was an aristocratic Arab woman who had been married twice before she met her third young and handsome husband, Abu al-Abbas (the future Caliph of the Abbasid dynasty). She married him at her own initiative after she sent her messenger with a proposal and a sum of money needed for the wedding. Al-Abbas, happily, accepted the offer, promising her, on oath, that he would never marry another woman or even take a concubine. Al-Abbas lived up to his word and did not have another wife until his demise. Umm Musa, an energetic lady of Arab descent, married Mansur before he assumed power as a second Caliph in Baghdad. In her marriage contract, she demanded that he would not marry another woman or take any concubines as long as she lived. And indeed he fulfilled his promise. Mansur was unable (despite desperate attempts on his part) to contract another marriage until she passed away. Finally, one can mention also the name of the Egyptian Islamist activist of this century, Zainab al-Ghazali. She married her first husband after she dictated in her marriage contract that he would help her to accomplish her mission (as leader of an Islamic movement). Failing to live up to her expectations, she divorced him and entered into a second marriage based on the same terms. See Ibn Sa'd, *al-Tabaqat*, Vol. 8, pp. 467–75; Nabia Abbott, *Two Queens of Baghdad*, Saqi Books, London, 1986, pp. 11–16; L. Ahmed, *Women and Gender in Islam*, op. cit., pp. 77–8 and p. 200.

31. L al-Faruqi, *Women, Muslim Society and Islam*, American Trust Publications, 1988, pp. 6–7.
32. *The Quran*, 4: 2.
33. *The Quran*, 30: 20.
34. A. Lemu, 'Women in Islam', in *Reading in Islam*, No. 6, Malaysia, 1979, p. 16.
35. *The Quran*, 2: 186.
36. A. Lemu, 'Women in Islam', op. cit., p. 16.
37. Cited in S. Murata, *The Tao of Islam*, op. cit., p. 172.
38. Regarding this point, the Prophet is reported to have said the following: 'When a Muslim man intends to come to his wife, God writes for him twenty good deeds and erases from him twenty evil deeds. When he takes her by the hand, God writes for him forty good deeds and erases from him forty evil deeds. When he kisses her, God writes for him sixty good deeds and erases from him sixty evil deeds. When he comes into her, God writes for him one hundred and twenty good deeds. When he stands up to make the ablution, God boasts of him to the angels and says "Look at My servant. He stands up in a cold night to wash himself of impurity, seeking the good pleasure of his hand. I bear witness to you that I have forgiven him".' Cited in Ibid., p. 174.
39. See H. Abd al-Ati, *Islam in Focus*, op. cit., pp. 117–18.
40. On this point Ibn Abbas is reported to have said 'I love to adorn myself for the woman just as I love that she adorn herself for me'. Cited in Ibid., p. 174.
41. *The Quran*, 2: 228.
42. *The Quran*, 4: 34.
43. M. Ulama, *The Pious Woman*, Young Men's Muslim Association, Port Elizabeth, South Africa, 1992, pp. 5–12.
44. Ibid., pp. 13–14 and p. 21.
45. Ibid., pp. 27–32.

WOMEN AND THE QUESTION OF POLYGAMY IN ISLAM

1. Hideko Iwai, *Islamic Society and Women in Islam*, the Institute of Middle East Studies, International University of Japan, Japan, 1985, pp. 6–8.
2. Ibid., pp. 8–10.
3. Ibid., pp. 7–12.
4. See Jamal J. Nasir, *The Status of Women Under Islamic Law*, Graham and Trotman, London, 1990.
5. Lois Lamya al-Faruqi, 'The Islamic Traditions and the Feminist Movement', op. cit., p. 136.

6. The term polygamy has been defined as the practice of marrying more than one wife or husband simultaneously. Also, it has been used interchangeably to refer to *Polyandry*, the habit in which one woman is married to several husbands; and *Polygany*, the custom in which one man is married to many wives. I used the term polygamy here to refer to the latter form of marriage, namely Polygany. From a historical perspective, both forms of marriage (Polyandry and Polygany) were practised in many parts of the world at certain times. However, with the passage of time, polyandry was weakened and gradually died out, while polygany managed to survive. The explanation given for the disintegration of polyandry is that the conditions or circumstances under which this kind of sexual behaviour is to prevail or survive are very difficult to obtain 'Polyandry is likely to prevail under such conditions as these: a very high sex ratio, lack of sexual jealousy, severe poverty, internalization of the conceptions of common property, benevolence with regard to sex, and insignificance of the economic output of women. It is very unlikely that these conditions will obtain in combination, long enough in a society to give rise to perpetual, institutionalized polyandry. Even if some of these conditions, such as poverty, prevail other conditions, e.g., sexual jealousy or acquisitiveness will most probably check the tendency toward total societal polyandry'. Cited from Hammudah Abd al-Ati, *The Family Structure in Islam*, op. cit., p. 99.

7. Al-Haj Mahomed Ullah Ibn S. Jung, *The Muslim Law of Marriage*, Law Publishing Company, Lahore, Pakistan, 1978, p. XXXI.

8. Thomas Patrick Hughes, *Dictionary of Islam*, W.H. Allen and Co, London, 1935, p. 462.

9. For further detail see A.M. al-Aqqad, *al-Mar'a Fi al-Quran al-Kareem*, Dar al-Hilal, Cairo, 1959, pp. 128–31.

10. Jamal A. Badawi, *Polygamy in Islamic Law*, American Trust Publications, Indiana, 1976, pp. 1–3.

11. Edward Westermarck, *The History of Human Marriage*, (5th Edition) Macmillan and Co., Ltd, London, 1925, p. 50.

12. It has been stated that despite the prohibition of the practice in the United States, the Mormons (members of the Church of Jesus Christ of Latter Day Saints founded by Joseph Smith in 1830 in Utah) have continued the custom secretly. Moreover, it is believed that there is no limitation as to the number of wives a Mormon can have; in general it varies from four to six but can even go up to twenty. See al-Hatimy, *Women in Islam*, op. cit., pp. 68–9.

13. Abeer Abu Saud, *Qatari Women: Past and Present*, Longman, London, 1984, pp. 88–9.

14. J. Badawi, *Polygamy in Islamic Law*, op. cit., pp. 2–3.

15. Doreen Ingrams, *The Awakened: Women in Iraq*, Third World Centre, London, 1983, p. 44.

16. It has been reported that the unlimited practice of polygamy continued among the Arabs even after the advent of Islam. The highly male-dominated society of ancient Arabia ensured that Arab males, even after they had converted to Islam, were in a position to carry on with the practice without any restraint. It was not until the revelation of the Quranic verse which limited the number of wives a man can have, that they were forced to reduce the number to the maximum required by the Divine Law. Here are a few examples which

illustrate the point: 'Nawfal bin Muawiya said: I had five wives and I told the Prophet about them; he told me, Choose any four you like and divorce the last one.' 'Umayr al-Asady said, I embraced Islam while I had eight wives. I told the Prophet about them and he told me, "Choose any four out of them".' Cited in al-Hatimy, *Women in Islam*, op. cit., p. 76.

17.   There is no doubt about the fact that the basic law of marriage in the Quran is that of monogamy. For example, if we look at the beginning of the creation we see that God created one man (Adam) and one woman (Eve), then He united them in the marriage bond to form the basic human unit in society. The foundation of the human race, therefore, is based on monogamous marriage rather than polygamous wedlock. Moreover, in the Quran there are many verses which explain clearly that the institution of marriage is founded on the basis of one man and one woman. For instance, Chapter 4, verse 1 says 'Men, have fear of your Lord, who created you from a single soul. From that soul He created its mate, and through them He bestrewed the earth with countless men and women'; Chapter 30, verse 20 states 'And of His signs is that He gave you wives (*azwaj* – meaning pairs) from among yourselves, that you might live in tranquillity with them, and put love and kindness in your hearts'. The above verses elucidate that the ideal and natural law of marriage in Islam is that of monogamy. For an elaborate discussion on this issue see Qamaruddin Khan, *Status of Women in Islam*, op. cit., pp. 16–18.

18.   Abeer Abu Saud, *Qatari Women: Past and Present*, op. cit., p. 90

19.   The circumstance in which the verse was revealed is given in the following explanatory statement by Muhammad Ali in his translation of the Quran. He states: 'This chapter (in which the verse appears) was revealed to guide the Muslims under the conditions which followed the battle of Ohud .... Now in that battle 70 men out of 700 Muslims had been slain, and this decimation had largely decreased the number of males, who, being the breadwinners, were the natural guardians and supporters of the females. The number was likely to suffer a still greater diminution in the battles which had yet to be fought, while the number of women would be increased by the addition of prisoners of war. Thus many orphans would be left in the charge of widows, who would find it difficult to procure the necessary means of support. Hence in the first verse of this chapter the Muslims are enjoined to respect the ties of relationship, and as they all came from a single ancestor breadth is introduced into the idea of relationship, inasmuch as they are told that they are all in fact related to each other. In the second verse the care of orphans is particularly enjoined. In the third verse we are told that if they could not do justice to the orphans, they might marry the widows, whose children would thus become their own children, and as the number of women was now much greater than the number of men, they were permitted to marry even two or three or four women. It would thus be clear that the permission to have more than one wife was given under the peculiar circumstances of the Muslim society then existing, and the Prophet's action in marrying widows, as well as the example of many of his companions, corroborates this statement. Marriage with orphan girls is also sanctioned in this passage, for there were the same difficulties in the case of orphan girls as in the case of widows, and the words are general'. Cited in Mohammad Mazheruddin Siddiqi, *Women in Islam*, op. cit., pp. 116–17.

20. *The Quran*, 4: 2.
21. *The Quran*, 4: 129.
22. There are some scholars who interpret the verses on polygamy in a wholly different way. They stress that the injunctions on polygamy are of a temporary nature intended in the first place to meet an urgent situation. Also, they insist that the rulings were revealed in a special historical context and consequently they are not a general licence for practising polygamy. In this respect Qamaruddin Khan offers the following interesting interpretation. He states: 'The permission given in the third verse (4: 3) is not an outright permission, nor a general licence to practise polygamy. It was given in a special historical situation brought about by a recent war, on account of which a large number of Muslim women and children had become orphans; there was an emergency, and there was no alternative to solve the problem of the orphans. Polygamy was the only solution therefore it was adopted. But the situation can not repeat itself, because the Muslims are now a world *Ummah*. If such emergencies arise again there may be several options available to solve the problem of widows and orphan girls; the permission was addressed only to the guardians. It was in the beginning of Islam in Medina. But now under the Shariah law, as well as the state law, no one however nearly related can claim any guardianship or authority over such widows and orphan girls; such orphans can be helped by state and social institutions and when they are economically rehabilitated they can look after their own affairs independently, and marry by their own choice, and save themselves from the hardship and indignity of polygamy; the permission, therefore, must be regarded as a temporary measure, and it can not be interpreted as a permanent law of marriage given in the Quran; the question of justice is also very important. In the third verse God has said: if you fear that you cannot be equitable to the several wives then have only one, or marry a slave-woman. Then in verse 129 of the same chapter, He says: you will not be able to be equitable between your wives, be you ever so eager; yet do not be altogether partial so that you leave her in suspense. Agreed that this is not an independent statement, but a continuation of the subject treated in verse (4: 3) in the beginning of the chapter. Here God has emphatically said that a man cannot be just to several wives, however much he might wish. In the same verse He says that one should not be too much partial to one wife and keep other wives suspended. From this the jurists have inferred that this verse has given a general permission of polygamy. But the fact is that polygamy is allowed, in this verse, to the guardians, as a lesser evil. God knew that they could not be just, yet He allowed them; for if He did not, the orphans would have suffered more grievously. And under no rules of exegesis can the verse be taken to mean a general permission of polygamy'. See Qamaruddin Khan, *Status of Women in Islam*, op. cit., pp. 21–2.
23. Muhammad Abduh, *al-Mar'a Fi al-Islam*, Compiled and introduced by Muhammad Amarah, Kitab al-Hilal, No. 347, November 1979, p. 33.
24. With regard to the special circumstances which necessitated the introduction of polygamy, they are the following: (1) the Muslim Community was in the process of establishing itself, therefore, it was in greater need for progeny to consolidate its foundation; (2) there was an urgent need to help the widows

and orphans who had lost their supporters and provide them with proper care and material welfare; (3) there was no welfare state system which could look after them and provide them with basic needs; (4) there was a need to regulate marriage ties which, at the time, were very loose and lax, and polygamy was a measure of regularisation and stability. See Hammudah Abd al-Ati, *The Family Structure in Islam*, op. cit., p. 121.

25.	Muhammad Abduh, *al-Mar'a Fi al-Islam*, op. cit., pp. 34–7.
26.	Turkey, immediately after the war of independence in 1924, banned polygamy altogether. This was done by replacing the religious law with a civil code.
27.	Jamal Badawi, *Polygamy in Islamic Law*, op. cit., p. 1.
28.	Eliz Sanasarian, 'Political Activism and Islamic Identity in Iran' in Lynne B. Iglitzin and Ruth Ross, *Women in the World 1975–1985*, (2nd edition), Santa Barbara, California, 1986, p. 215.
29.	Malik Ram Baveja, *Women in Islam*, op. cit., p. 46.
30.	Ibid., p. 46.
31.	Ibid., p. 47.
32.	Hammudah Abd al-Ati, *The Family Structure in Islam*, op. cit., p. 118.
33.	S. Saeed, 'The Legal Status of Muslim Women', *The Islamic Quarterly*, Vol. XXIV, No. 1 and 2, 1980, p. 16.
34.	Malik Ram Baveja, *Women in Islam*, op. cit., p. 47.
35.	For further detail see al-Sayyid Sabiq, *Fiqh al-Sunnah*, Dar al-kitab al-arabi, Beirut, Vol. 2, 1977, pp. 112–14.
36.	Abeer Abu Saud, *Qatari Women: Past and Present*, op. cit., pp. 89–90.
37.	Hammudah Abd al-Ati, *The Family Structure in Islam*, op. cit., p. 120.
38.	For an elabrate discussion on this issue see Ahmad al-Ghandur, *al-Ahwal Al-Shakhsiyyah fi al-tashr' al-Islami*, Maktabat al-falah, Kuwait, 1982, pp. 143–5.
39.	Jamal A. Badawi, *Polygamy in Islamic Law*, op. cit., pp. 7–9.
40.	The whole question of strong sexual urge, in my opinion is nonsense. There are more fundamental things in life than having constant or unstoppable sex. Besides, it contradicts the Islamic principle that Muslims have to control and not be controlled by, their sexual desires. After all, sex is only one aspect or reason for entering into a marriage.
41.	See, Abdur Rahman Doi, *Women in Shariah*, op. cit., p. 52.
42.	See Haleh Afshar, 'Women, Marriage and the State in Iran' in Haleh Afshar, *Women, State, and Ideology*, Macmillan, London, 1987, pp. 78–81.
43.	M. Abdul-Rauf, *The Islamic View of Women and the Family*, op. cit., p. 119.

FEMALE CIRCUMCISION: RELIGIOUS OBLIGATION OR CULTURAL DEVIATION?

1.	Anne Cloudsley, *Women of Omdurman, Life, Love and the Cult of Virginity*, Ethnographica, London, 1983, p. 120.
2.	Dior Diop, 'Tackling the Problem' in *Health*, 26 April–2 May 1993, p. 685.
3.	It has been stated that at one time the mutilation was performed by men rather than women: 'a strong man standing behind the girl to hold her while

the surgeon who operates stands in front of her'; 'the operator who is more often than not a barber, uses his fingers dipped in ash to get hold of the clitoris, which he pulls several times from back to front so as to cut it off with a single stroke of the razor, when it appears as a simple fibre of skin'. See Otto Meinardus, *Christian Egypt: Faith and Life*, The American University Press, Cairo, 1970, p. 333.

4. For an interesting account of the terrifying personal experiences of women who undergo such mutilation, See N. El-Saadawi, *The Hidden Face of Eve: Women in the Arab World*, Zed Books, London, 1980, pp. 7–8.

5. *Foundation for Women's Health, Research and Development*, (FORWARD), the Information Office, London, April 1994.

6. Ibid.

7. Mrs Walker considers it as 'a heinous form of patriarchal oppression, characterized by the feeling of being overpowered and thoroughly dominated by those you are duty bound to respect', *The Times*, March 21, 1994, p. 48.

8. *The Guardian*, 25 April 1994.

9. *The Voice of America*, Arabic Section, April 1994.

10. *The Times*, op. cit.

11. *Forward*, Information Office, op. cit.

12. Personal interview, Yemen, April 1994.

13. For more information see A. El-Dareer, *Woman, Why do You Weep?*, Zed Press, London, 1982, pp. 23–5.

14. *Forward*, Information Office, op. cit.

15. Some add other forms of mutilation to the list: (1) *Intermediate Infibulation* which consists of different kinds of mutilation. In one case the clitoris is cut and the face of the labia minora stiffened so as to facilitate stitching. In other cases, the labia minora are cut, the insides of the labia majora are erased and sewed leaving the clitoris intact buried underneath; (2) *Unclassified*, these types of mutilation involve scarification of the clitoral hood, cuts into the clitoris and labia minora as well as into the vagina. See Efua Dorkenoo, *Cutting the Rose, Female Genital Mutilation: The Practice and its Prevention*, Minority Rights Publications, London, 1994, pp. 5–8. Also, see Asma El-Dareer, *Woman Why do You Weep? Circumcision and its Consequences*, op. cit., pp. 3–5.

16. Although this kind of circumcision has been regarded as mild and soft, in reality and from a medical viewpoint, it is a form of mutilation 'Any definitive and irremediable removal of a healthy organ is a mutilation. The female external genital organ normally is constituted by the vulva, which comprises the labia majora, the labia minora or nymphae, and the clitoris covered by its prepuce, in front of the vestibule to the urinary meatus and the vaginal orifice. Their constitution in female humans is genetically programmed and is identically reproduced in all embryos and in all races. The vulva is an integral part of the natural inheritance of humanity. When normal, there is absolutely no reason, medical, moral, or aesthetic, to suppress all or any part of these exterior genital organs'. Cited in Dorkenoo, *Cutting the Rose*, op. cit., p. 4.

17. E. Dorkenoo and S. Elworthy, *Female Genital Mutilation: Proposals for Change*, Minority Rights Group, London, 1992, p. 7.

18. Alin. Qrunbum, 'The Political Economy of Infibulation' in *Journal for Sudanese Studies*, Khartoum University Press, Sudan, 1991, p. 10.

19. This has been confirmed by the following statement from Aetius of Amid (IVth, century AD) the court-physician at Byzantium. He states: 'And, in addition, with certain of the women their clitoris increases in growth and becomes unseemly and shameful, but also being continually rubbed by their garments it excites them and rouses the desire for copulation; wherefore, on account of its increased size, the Egyptians determined to take it off, especially at the time when girls were ready to be married. The surgery is accomplished in this manner. They cause the girl to be seated on a stool, and a strong young man standing behind her, places his forearms beneath her thighs and buttocks, holding fast her legs and her whole body. The operator standing in front of her seizes with a wide-mouthed forceps her clitoris, pulling it out with his left hand, whilst with his right hand he cuts off with the teeth of the forceps'. Also, Ambrosius, a physician of the Graeco-Roman world states 'Moreover, the Egyptians circumcise the males in their 14th year, and the females among them are brought to be circumcised in the same year, because it is clear that from that year the passion of men begins to burn, and the menstruations of women have their beginnings'. Cited in Otto Meinardus, *Christian Egypt: Faith and Life*, op. cit., pp. 324–5.

20. The Copts in Egypt believe that the practice of female circumcision spread among them because of the victory of the circumcised, i.e. the Jews. See O. Meinardus, op. cit., p. 327.

21. It has been stated that the first account of infibulation was found in the writings of the historian Pietro Bembo first published in 1551 or 1552. He explains: 'Now left the other countries, sailed into the Red Sea and visited several countries, inhabited by blacks, excellent men, brave in war. Among these people the private parts of the girls are sewn together immediately after their birth, but in a way not to hinder the urinary ways. When the girls have become adult, they are given away in marriage in this condition and the husband's first measure is to cut open with a knife the solidly consolidated private parts of the virgin. Among the barbarous peoples an indubitable virginity at the marriage is held in such high esteem'. See Anne Cloudsley, *Women of Omdurman*, op. cit., p. 111.

22. Dior Diop, 'Tackling the Problem', op. cit.

23. In reality, almost all African countries practise female circumcision. A recent survey in *The Times* estimated that 98 per cent of women are circumcised in Djibouti and Somalia, 90 per cent in Ethiopia, 80 per cent in Sudan and 75 per cent in Mali. See, *The Times*, March 1994.

24. Olayinka Koso-Thomas, *The Circumcision of Women: A Strategy for Eradication*, Zed Books, London, 1987, p. 17.

25. Pain can also result because of the raw wound and the difficulty in passing urine, especially in the Pharaonic type of circumcision.

26. This is due to severe circumcision and can be found only in the intermediate and pharaonic types. Some retain urine right from the first day of the operation, others at a later stage, especially after infection. They require urgent relief and this is usually done by decircumcision. See Asma El-Dareer, *Woman Why do You Weep?*, op. cit., p. 32.

27. This is the most common condition among circumcised women, especially those with intermediate and pharaonic circumcision, and it could result in serious psychological implications: on the mens' side it could lead to frustration and impotence; on the womens' side it could result in them hating sex and having no pleasure in their sexual life. The only treatment for this condition is decircumcision. A. El-Dareer, op. cit., pp. 35–6.

28. Olayinka Koso-Thomas, *The Circumcision of Women: A Strategy for Eradication*, op. cit., pp. 25–8.

29. Personal interview, Yemen, April 1994.

30. A. El-Dareer, *Woman Why do You Weep?*, op. cit., pp. 36–7.

31. The following message indicates this clear connection: 'While in Malawi a couple of months ago I came across the story of a 14 year-old girl of the Yao tribe that inhabits land in the southern end of the country. She was diagnosed HIV-positive although she was a virgin. Blame was laid on the fact that during tribal circumcision the same razor would be used on any number of children at the same time. The solution the chief offered to take up was that in future each child was to bring their own razor'. Cited in Efua Dorkenoo, *Cutting the Rose*, op. cit., p. 14.

32. Abstract of the book by S.R. Erlander, *The Cause of AIDS*, England, 1993 – the abstract was obtained from the Institute for Research and Studies, Ministry of Health, Yemen, April 1994.

33. For more information see O.K. Thomas, *The Circumcision of Women*, op. cit. Also see E. Dorkenoo and S. Elworthy, *Female Genital Mutilation*, op. cit.

34. Among certain communities where female genital mutilation is practised there is a deep cultural belief that an uncircumcised organ is ugly and disgusting. Therefore, if the female genitals are left uncircumcised they would grow and dangle between their legs which make them repulsive to men. Remarks such as 'you are not a proper woman' or 'you are like a man' are very often used to describe an uncircumcised woman. Efua Dorkenoo, *Cutting the Rose*, op. cit., p. 34.

35. Personal interview, Yemen, April 1994.

36. It is largely believed, especially among advocates of the practice, that the partial or complete removal of the clitoris, which is considered as the focal point of sexual excitement, is essential to protect pre-martial chastity. Otto Meinardus, op. cit., p. 334. Also, it is widely accepted among the communities concerned that female circumcision, particularly infibulation, would make the rape of virgins highly unlikely. A popular Sudanese saying runs as follows: 'A Sudanese girl is like a water-melon because there is no way in' confirms this belief. Anne Cloudsley, op. cit., pp. 117–8.

37. Personal interview, Yemen, April 1994.

38. Personal interview, Yemen, April 1994.

39. Anne Cloudsley, *Women of Omdurman*, op. cit., pp. 116–20.

40. N. El-Saadawi, *The Hidden Face of Eve: Women in the Arab World*, op. cit., p. 35.

41. Personal interview, Yemen, April 1994.

42. Personal interview, Yemen, April 1994.

43. Regarding male circumcision, it has long been considered, in all Muslim countries, as a religious tradition. It is believed that circumcision was

common among all prophets and that Abraham was the first prophet to be circumcised. The Quran (implicitly) refers to the practice of male circumcision. For example, Chapter 2, verse 122 states: 'When his Lord put Ibrahim to the proof by enjoining on him certain commandments and Ibrahim fulfilled them, He said: I have appointed you a leader of mankind'. Also, 16: 123 says 'Then we revealed to you: follow the faith of saintly Ibrahim: he was no polytheist'. Hence it is believed that one of these commands is circumcision which Ibrahim had accomplished. In the *Hadith* literature we find the following authentic *Hadiths* which support the practice of male circumcision: 'Five norms define *fitrah*: shaving of the pubic hair, circumcision, moustache trimming, armpit depilation and nail clipping'. Someone came to the Prophet and declared his conversion before him; the Prophet told him: 'Shave off your unbeliever's hair and be circumcised'; 'The Prophet said: let him who becomes a Muslim be circumcised, even if he is old'; once the prophet was asked if an uncircumcised man could go to pilgrimage. The Prophet answered: 'Not as long as he is not circumcised'. All cited in Sami Aldeeb Abu-Sahlieh, *To Mutilate in the Name of Jehovah or Allah, Legitimisation of Male and Female Circumcision*, Unpublished Research, Institute of Canon Law, University of Human Sciences, Strasbourg, France, 1994, p. 9.

44.   Another version puts it as follows 'Reduce but do not destroy. This is enjoyable to the woman and preferable to the man'. Cited in Asma El-Dareer, Woman *Why do You Weep?*, op. cit., p. 72.

45.   All cited in Sami Aldeeb Abu-Sahlieh, *To Mutilate in the Name of Jehovah or Allah*, op. cit., pp. 9–10.

46.   The position of the four schools of law on this subject varies from one school to another. For example, the Shafeites maintain that it is a duty for both males and females; the Hanifites and the Malakites regard the circumcision of both boys and girls as commendable; while the Hanbelites hold that circumcision is mandatory upon men and only advisable for women. It must be stressed that all four schools refer to the Sunnah type of circumcision which they define as the 'removal of the lower part of the protruding skin at the top-part of the vagina'. Both excision and infibulation have never been approved of by any of them. The definition is cited in Anne Cloudsley, *Women of Omdurman*, op. cit., p. 103.

47.   Cited in Sami Aldeeb Abu-Sahlieh, *To Mutilate in the Name of Jehovah or Allah*, op. cit., p. 10.

48.   Cited in Ibid., p. 10.

49.   Renee Saurel eloquently states the position: 'The Koran, contrary to Christianism and Judaism, permits and recommends that the woman be given physical and psychological pleasure, pleasure found by both partners during the act of love. Forcibly split, torn, and severed tissues are neither conducive to sensuality nor to the blessed feeling given and shared when participating in the quest for pleasure and the escape from pain'. Cited in Aldeeb, op. cit., p. 11. Also, the Quran, 32: 6, says 'Such is He, the Knower of the visible and the invisible. He is the Mighty One, the Merciful, who created all things in the best way. He first created man from clay, then bred his offspring from a drop of paltry fluid. He then moulded him and breathed into him of His spirit. He gave you eyes and ears, and hearts; yet you are

seldom thankful'. Hence, female circumcision can be viewed as a deliberate attempt to tamper with the perfect Divine creation.

50. See al-Sayyid Sabiq, *Fiqh al-Sunnah*, Dar al-Fikr, Beirut, 1992.
51. Abdullah. Alwan, *The Education of Children in Islam*, Assalam Press, Cairo, 1983, p. 113.
52. See E.K. Hicks, *Infibulation: Female Mutilation in Islamic North Eastern Africa*, Transaction Publishers, New Brunswick, New Jersey, USA, 1993, pp. 24–5.
53. El-Saadawi writes 'It has very often been proclaimed that Islam is at the root of female circumcision, and is also responsible for the under-privileged and backward situation of women in Egypt and the Arab countries. Such a contention is not true ... Religion, if authentic in the principles it stands for, aims at truth, equality, justice, love and a healthy wholesome life for all people, whether men or women. There can be no true religion that aims at disease, mutilation of the bodies of female children, and amputation of an essential part of their reproductive organs. If religion comes from God, how can it order man to cut off an organ created by Him as long as that organ is not diseased or deformed? God does not create the organs of the body haphazardly without a plan. It is not possible that He should have created the clitoris in woman's body only in order that it be cut off at an early stage in life. This is a contradiction into which neither true religion nor the Creator could possibly fall. If God has created the clitoris as a sexually sensitive organ, whose sole function seems to be the procurement of sexual pleasure for women, it follows that He also considers such pleasure for women as normal and legitimate, and therefore as an integral part of mental health'. See El-Saadawi, *The Hidden Face of Eve*, op. cit., pp. 41–2.
54. The Quran encourages Muslims to look after their mental and physical well-being. It also debars them from inflicting harm on themselves. Chapter 2, verse 194 says 'Give for the cause of Allah and do not with your own hands cast yourselves into destruction. Be charitable; Allah loves the charitable'. As medical science has proved beyond doubt that female circumcision is damaging and detrimental to women's health, it is therefore in line with the Divine instruction to avoid causing any destruction to yourselves by your own hands. Shaltut, the former Sheikh of *al-Azhar* in Cairo advocates the same attitude: 'Islamic legislation provides a general principle, namely that should meticulous and careful examination of certain issues prove that it is definitely harmful or immoral, then it should be legitimately stopped to put an end to this damage or immorality. Therefore, since the harm of excision has been established, excision of the clitoris of females is not a mandatory obligation, nor is it a Sunnah'. Cited in Efua Dorkenoo, *Cutting the Rose*, op. cit., p. 37.
55. Apparently there exist many *fatwas* before the last one. Those *fatwas* show the inconsistency in the position of *al-Azhar*. For example, the first *fatwa* was issued in 1949 in which the practice was discouraged. Another one was passed in 1951. It did not favour the idea of abolishing the practice and advised people to continue with it. The third *fatwa* was issued in 1981, clearly opposing any attempt to abandon the practice. See Aldeeb, op. cit., p. 15.
56. The *Voice of America*, Arabic section, 12 April, 1995.

ISLAM AND WOMEN'S INHERITANCE

1. *The Quran*, 4: 7.
2. Al-Tabari, *Tafsir al-Quran*, op. cit., Vol. 4, p. 262.
3. Ibid., pp. 3–6.
4. Ibid., p. 306.
5. Ibid., p. 306.
6. *The Quran*, 4: 19.
7. *Al-Tabari*, op. cit., Vol. 4, p. 306.
8. Ibid., p. 309.
9. *Al-Tabari*, op. cit., Vol. 5, p. 300.
10. *The Quran*, 4: 2.
11. *The Quran*, 4: 6.
12. *The Quran*, 4: 10.
13. *The Quran*, 2: 214.
14. *The Quran*, 4: 35.
15. *The Quran*, 6: 152.
16. Al-Tabari, *Tafsir*, op. cit., Vol. 4, p. 275 and p. 291; also Vol. 5, pp. 299–3.
17. *The Quran*, 4: 127.
18. *The Quran*, 4: 12.
19. A. Engineer, *The Rights of Women in Islam*, op. cit., p. 70.
20. *The Quran*, 4: 10.
21. Al-Tabari, Vol. 4, p. 270.
22. A. Engineer, op. cit., p. 71.
23. Cited in Ibid., p. 72.
24. *The Quran*, 4: 7.
25. Ibn al-Arabi, *Ahkam al-Quran*, Dar al-Kutub al-'Ilmiya, Beirut, Vol. 1, 1988, p. 431.
26. Personal interview, June 1995.

THE DISSOLUTION OF MARRIAGE IN ISLAM

1. Cited from H. Abd al-Ati, *The Family Structure in Islam*, op. cit., p. 217.
2. *The Quran*, 33: 36.
3. *The Quran*, 4: 19.
4. *The Quran*, 4: 19.
5. *A Concise Encyclopaedia of Islam*, Cyril Glasse, Stacey International, London, 1989, p. 100.
6. M.K. Adamu, *The Islamic Notion of Marriage and Divorce*, Joeart Productions, Laranto, Nigeria, 1987, p. 62.
7. K. Jan Dorph 'Islamic Law in Contemporary North Africa: A Study of the Laws of Divorce in the Maghreb', in Azizah al-Hibri (ed.), *Women and Islam*, Pergamon Press, London, 1982, p. 172.
8. M.K. Adamu, *The Islamic Notion of Marriage and Divorce*, op. cit., p. 64.
9. K. Jan Dorph 'Islamic Law in Contemporary North Africa', op. cit., p. 173.
10. A. Ezzati, *An Introduction to Shi'i Islamic Law and Jurisprudence*, Ashrat Press, Lahore, Pakistan, 1976, p. 148.

11. *The Quran*, 4: 35.
12. N.J. Coulson, *A History of Islamic Law*, Edinburgh University Press, 1964, p. 211.
13. M. Abduh, *Women and Islam*, op. cit., p. 79.
14. Ibid., p. 79.
15. Ibid., pp. 78–9.
16. Ibid., p. 83.
17. N.J. Coulson, *A History of Islamic Law*, op. cit., p. 211.
18. Ibid., p. 211.
19. Cited in A.A. Engineer, *The Rights of Women in Islam*, op. cit., p. 122.
20. *The Quran*, 2: 229.
21. *The Quran*, 2: 230.
22. A woman, however, can re-marry her former husband if she so wishes after her waiting period runs out. This happens when the husband gives his first divorce and leaves the waiting period of the wife to lapse without pronouncing the third one; hence leaving the possibility of the spouses to re-marry if they decide to do so. The Quran says, 'If a man has divorced his wife and she has reached the end of her waiting period, do not prevent her from re-marrying her husband if they have come to an honourable agreement. This is enjoined on everyone of you who believes in Allah and the Last Day; it is more honourable for you and more chaste. Allah knows, but you do not' (2: 231). It has been said that this verse was revealed when the sister of Ma'qal bin Yasar was divorced by her husband. He pronounced one divorce and let the waiting period lapse without pronouncing a third one. However, when the *idda* (waiting time) expired, he regretted his action and wished to take his wife back. The wife was also willing to go back to her husband but her brother, Ma'qal, was unhappy about her decision. Hence, this verse was revealed to clarify the situation. See S. Qutb, *Fi Zilal al-Qur'an*, Dar al-Shuruq, Beirut/Cairo, 1987, Vol. 1, p. 253.
23. This is based on the following *Hadith*: Abdullah ibn Umar divorced his wife while she was menstruating. His father, Umar ibn al-Khattab, sought advice from the Prophet, who said, 'Order him (your son) to take her back and keep her till she is clean from her menses and then to wait till she gets her next period and becomes clean again, whereupon, if he wishes to keep her, he can do so, and if he wishes to divorce her he can divorce her, before having sexual intercourse with her; and that is the prescribed period which Allah has fixed for the women meant to be divorced'. See Bukhari, *The Book of Divorce*, p. 907.
24. The Quran says: 'If you (believers) divorce your wives, divorce them at (the end) of their waiting period. Compute their waiting period and have fear of Allah, your Lord'. (65: 1).
25. The Quran says: 'When you have divorced your wives and they have reached the end of their waiting period, either retain them in honour or let them go with kindness. But you shall not retain them in order to harm them or to wrong them. Whoever does this wrongs his own soul'. (2: 231). Also, Chapter 65 verse 2 says: 'When they have reached their prescribed time, either keep them honourably or part with them honourably. Call to witness two honest men among you and give your testimony before Allah. Whoever believes in Allah and the Last Day is exhorted to do this'.

26. Here the Quran says, 'Do not expel them (wives) from their homes or let them go away unless they commit a proven immorality. Such are the bounds set by Allah; he that transgresses Allah's bounds wrongs his own soul' (65: 1).

27. The Quran instructs the husband to secure her future. It says, 'Reasonable provision should also be made for divorced women. That is incumbent on righteous men' (2: 240).

28. L. al-Faruqi, *Women, Muslim Society and Islam*, op. cit., p. 7.

29. A. Rahim, *Muhammadan Jurisprudence*, Indus Publications, Lahore, Pakistan, 1968, p. 335.

30. Ahmed Shukri, *Muhammadan Law of Marriage and Divorce*, AMS Press, New York, 1966, pp. 97–8.

31. Ibid., pp. 98–9.

32. A. Rahim, *Muhammadan Jurisprudence*, op. cit., p. 337.

33. Ahmed Shukri, *Muhammadan Law on Marriage and Divorce*, op. cit., p. 99.

34. This is based on the following: 'The wife of Rifa'a al-Qurazi came (to the Prophet) and said: O Allah's Messenger! Rifa'a divorced me irrevocably. After him I married Zubair al-Qurazi, who proved to be impotent. (The Prophet) said to her, 'perhaps you want to return to Rifa'a? Nay (you cannot return to Rifa'a) until you enjoy the sexual relation (consummate your marriage) with him (Zubair) and he with you'. Bukhari, pp. 908–9.

35. A. Adamu, *The Islamic Notion of Marriage and Divorce*, op. cit., p. 67.

36. L. Badawi, 'Islam' in J. Holm and J. Bowker (eds), *Women in Religion*, Pinter Publishers, London, 1994, p. 106.

37 A. Rahim, *Muhammadan Jurisprudence*, op. cit., p. 338.

38. J. Nasir, *The Status of Women under Islamic Law*, op. cit., p. 78.

39. If the husband refuses to give his consent, she has the right to take him to court.

40. A. Mawdudi, *The Law of Marriage and Divorce in Islam*, Islamic Book Publishers, Kuwait, second edition, 1993, pp. 35–6.

41. For more discussion on *khula*, see Musa Ali Ajetunmobi, 'The Concept of Kuhla and Examination of its Cases in Nigerian Courts of Shariah Jurisdiction', in *Islam and the Modern Age*, Vol. XIX, No. 4, Nov 1988, pp. 263–84.

42. Bukhari, *The Book of Divorce*, p. 910. Also, another incident: 'Barira's husband was a slave called Mughith. (He used to go) behind Barira and (weep) with his tears flowing down his beard (because she was demanding *khula*). The Prophet said to Abbas: 'O Abbas! Are you not astonished at the love of Mughith for Barira and the hatred of Barira for Mughith?' The Prophet then said to Barira, 'Why don't you return to him?' She said, 'Do you order me to do so?' He said, 'No, I only intercede for him'. She said, 'I am not in need of him'. Ibid., p. 911.

43. H. al-Ati, *The Family Structure in Islam*, op. cit., p. 244.

44. L. al-Faruqi, *Women, Muslim Society and Islam*, op. cit., p. 8.

45. M. Khadduri, *Islamic Jurisprudence*, The Johns Hopkins Press, Baltimore, 1961, p. 147.

46. The oaths are based on Chapter 24 verse 6, which says, 'And those who accuse their wives and have no witnesses except themselves, let each of them testify by swearing four times by Allah that his charge is true, calling

down in the fifth time upon himself the curse of Allah if he is lying. But they shall spare her the punishment if she swears four times by Allah that his charge is false and calls down Allah's wrath upon herself if it be true'.

47. A. Rahim, *Muhammadan Jurisprudence*, op. cit., p. 339.

48. It must be stressed here that there are two other unusual forms of divorce under Islamic Law: these are known as *Iha* and *Zihar*. *Iha* occurs when a man swears that he would not have sexual intercourse with his wife for at least four months. If, in the meanwhile, he does not break his vow and resume conjugal relations, the legal impact of his action would be a single irrevocable divorce. In the case of *Zihar*, the husband compares his wife to the back of, for example, his mother, or other female relatives with whom sexual relations are prohibited, thus making intercourse with his wife unlawful until he atones for his misconduct. See A. Rahim, op. cit., pp. 338–9 and A. Shukri, op. cit., pp. 116–21.

WOMEN AND POLITICAL ACTION

1. *The Quran*, 2: 286.

2. There are many verses in the Quran which clearly indicate that *Khilafa* includes both men and women. For example, Chapter 3, verse 194 states 'Their Lord answers them, saying: I will deny no man or woman among you the reward of their labours. You are the offspring of one another'. Chapter 16, verse 98 says 'We shall reward the steadfast according to their noblest deeds. Be they men or women, those that embrace the faith and do what is right we will surely grant a happy life, we shall reward them according to their noblest actions'. And again Chapter 49, verse 13: '(O people) we have created you from a male and a female, and made you into nations and tribes that you might get to know one another. The noblest of you in Allah's sight is the most righteous of you. Allah is Wise and All-knowing'.

3. Also, Chapter 3, verse 105 says 'Let there become of you a nation that shall call for righteousness, enjoin justice, and forbid evil – such (people) shall surely triumph'. In this verse there is a clear cut instruction for both men and women to become actively involved in the politics of their society and are promised rewards if they do so and succeed.

4. We refer here to the role played by Khadija, the first wife of the Prophet at the initial stage of his mission: comforting him, re-assuring him and believing, later on, in his message, thus becoming the first woman to embrace Islam. Listen to what she had to say to him when he came to her with his heart beating violently after he had received the first divine revelation: 'O Khadija cover me, cover me ... I fear that something may happen to me'. Khadija replied: never! By Allah, Allah will never disgrace you. You keep good relations with your kith and kin, help the poor and the destitute, serve your guests generously and assist the deserving calamity-afflicted ones'. See Bukhari, *The Book of Revelation*, pp. 50–1. Also, it is important to mention the crucial role played by Asma bint Abu Bakr in planning and facilitating the secret migration of the Prophet with his closest friend Abu Bakr from Mecca to Medina; that migration which changed the whole history of the

Islamic mission. See Muhammad Amarah, *Is Islam the Solution? Why and How?*, Dar al-Shuruq, Cairo, 1995, p. 143.

5. Among the names of the many women who had to put up with abuse and maltreatment was Sumayya, the mother of the famous companion Ammar ibn Yasir; she was brutally murdered by Abu Jahl for refusing to abandon her belief. She is regarded as the first (woman) martyr in Islam.

6. There is a long list of names of Muslim women who fled their homes in order to keep and cling to their new faith. Here are a few examples: 'Umm Khalid bint Khalid (said) when I came from Ethiopia (to al-Madina) I was a young girl. Allah's Messenger made me wear a sheet having marks on it. Allah's Messenger was rubbing those marks with his hands saying Sanah! Sanah! (i.e. good, good)'. Also, as narrated by Asma bint Abu Bakr: 'I migrated to Medina while I was at full term of pregnancy and alighted at Quba where I gave birth to him (her son Abdullah bin Zubair). Then I brought him to the Prophet and put him in his lap .... Then the Prophet invoked for Allah's Blessings on him, and he was the first child born amongst the emigrants'. See *Bukhari*, p. 736; also pp. 752–3.

7. Chapter 61, verse 12 speaks of the allegiance which was given by women to Muhammad. It says, 'O Prophet, if believing women come to you and pledge themselves to associate in worship nothing with Allah, to commit neither theft, nor adultery, nor child-murder, to utter no monstrous false-hoods (concerning the fatherhood of their children), and to disobey you in nothing just, accept their allegiance and implore Allah to forgive them. Allah is Forgiving and Merciful'.

8. This is based on a *Hadith* which states, 'It is obligatory for one to listen to and obey (a Muslim ruler's orders) unless these orders involve one in dis-obedience (to Allah); but if an act of disobedience (to Allah) is imposed, one should not listen to or obey it'. See *Bukhari*, p. 604.

9. The Prophet said, 'He who obeys me (the Prophet) obeys Allah, and he who disobeys me disobeys Allah. He who obeys the Muslim chief, obeys me, and he who disobeys the Muslim chief, disobeys me. The Imam is like a shelter for whose safety the Muslims should fight and where they should seek protection. If the Imam orders people to be dutiful to Allah and fear Him and rules justly, then he will be rewarded for that, and if he does the opposite, then he will be responsible for that'. See *Bukhari*, p. 605.

10. In declaring her loyalty to Muhammad, listen to what Hind bint Utba had to say: 'O Allah's Messenger (before I embraced Islam) there was no family on the surface of the earth I wished to see in degradation more than I did your family, but today there is no family on the surface of the earth I wish to see honoured more than I do yours'. See *Bukhari*, p. 733.

11. Contrary to the popular conception, there is no difference in either the style or the content between the *bay'a* of women and that of men. In most cases the Prophet recited the same formula for men as he did for women. For example: The Prophet said (to men) 'Give me the bay'a (pledge) for: Not to join anything in worship along with Allah, not to steal, not to commit illegal sexual intercourse, not to kill your children, not to utter slander intentionally forging falsehood (i.e. by making illegal children belonging to their husbands or not to accuse an innocent person and to spread such accusation among people), not to be disobedient (when

ordered) to do *Maruf* (good deeds) (so men gave the *Baia* (pledge) for these)'. *Bukhari*, pp. 62–3. This formula is exactly the same as the women's one; compare with note 7.

12. See H.R. Ezzat, *Women and Political Action: An Islamic Perspective* (in Arabic), the International Institute of Islamic Thought, Virginia, 1995, pp. 120–6.
13. *The Quran*, 3: 156.
14. *The Quran*, 42: 35.
15. H. Ezzat, op. cit., pp. 142–9.
16. The incident referred to was called the pact of Hudaybiyya, a peace treaty which was signed under difficult conditions. Many Muslims, especially the prominent companions of the Prophet, such as Ali and Umar, felt that they were outmanoeurvred by their enemies; also, they thought that the Prophet was too lenient by virtue of the fact that he had made unwarranted concessions. For example, the Prophet agreed, under pressure from Quraysh, not to begin the treaty with the phrase, 'in the name of God' (as the Muslims wished), nor sign the treaty under the name of 'Muhammad, the Messenger of God'. Although they planned to visit Mecca and perform the Umra (lesser pilgrimage), they were forced to postpone it to the following year. More importantly, the treaty made it conditional that if a person from the pagan side converted to Islam and sought refuge in the Muslim side, the Muslims were obliged to return him to the pagans of Mecca. But if a Muslim changed loyalty and went over to the Meccans, the Meccans were under no obligation to hand him over to the Muslims. The companions could not comprehend the reasons behind the acceptance, by the Prophet, of such rigid terms and questioned the validity of the treaty. This was demonstrated by the fact that when the Prophet ordered his followers to perform the rituals of shaving their heads and sacrificing their animals without entering Mecca, they disobeyed him. He repeated his order three times but to no avail. Saddened by their negative attitudes, he went to his wife Umm Salama and told her the whole story, asking if she thought that there was a way out of the predicament. Umm Salama with her usual shrewdness and sagacity suggested to him that he should himself proceed and perform the rituals, believing that once he performed them, the Muslims would then change their attitude and follow his actions and indeed that was what happened. See K. Siddique, *The Struggle of Muslim Women*, Singapore, 1988, pp. 37–42. Also, see Bukhari, *The Book of Conditions*, pp. 565–74.
17. The Quran encourages both able men and women to become well-versed in the knowledge of their religion and to attain a position of being a Mufti (deliverer of formal legal opinions) so that they could help the less fortunate ones understand the rules of their religion. The Quran says in Surah 16, verse 39 'Ask the knowledgeable if you do not know'. Also, Surah 9, verse 122, 'Some should stay behind to instruct themselves in religion and admonish the others when they return, so that they may take heed'.
18. We refer here to the incident in which Aisha heard Abu Hurayra narrating a *Hadith* slightly different from the one she heard from the Prophet. So she criticised him and corrected the way he narrated the *Hadith*. See K. Siddique, op. cit., pp. 46–50.
19. Ibid., p. 50.

20. Abdul Halim Abu Shaqqa, *The Liberation of Women at the Time of the Prophecy*, part two, op. cit., pp. 432–3.
21. Also, during the battle of Maisan, while the Muslim troops were fighting the Persians, a woman by the name of Arda suggested that other women make flags out of some of their clothes and march toward the battlefield. The Persians, thinking that more troops were sent to help the Muslims, fled from the battlefield leaving the Muslims in a victorious position. See H. Krausen, 'Women and Politics', *Q-News*, 26 July–1 August 1996, p. 9.
22. Here we refer to the *Hadith* narrated by Umm Atiyya regarding the participation of menstruating women in the two Eid festivals. She said 'I heard Allah's Messenger (say) that the unmarried virgins and the mature girls and the menstruating women should come out and participate in the good deeds as well as invocations of the faithful believers but the menstruating women should keep away from the Musalla – praying place'. See *Bukhari*, p. 148.
23. See, for example, the *Hadith* which states that 'The Prophet stood up to offer the prayer of the Id-ul-Fitr. He first offered the prayer and then delivered the Khutba. After finishing it he got down (from the pulpit) and went towards the women and advised them while he was leaning on Bilal's hand'. See *Bukhari*, Vol. 2, p. 50.
24. See, for example, the *Hadith* which says 'The Prophet said if the wife of any one of you asks permission (to go to the mosque) do not forbid her'. Also, the Prophet said 'If your women ask permission to go to the mosque at night allow them'. The following statement indicates, 'when Allah's Messenger finished the Fajr prayer, the women would leave covered in their sheets and were not recognised owing to the darkness'. See *Bukhari*, Vol. 1, p. 459, and, pp. 456–7.
25. See the following statement: 'Some women requested the Prophet to fix a day for them as the men were taking all his time. On that he promised them one day for religious lessons and commandments', *Bukhari*, Vol. 1, p. 80.
26. This self-awareness was clearly demonstrated by Umm Salama when on one occasion, while her assistant was combing her hair, she heard the Prophet calling for Jami'a prayer: 'O people!' Umm Salama promptly stopped her so that she could answer the Prophet's call. Her assistant then told her, but the Prophet called men not women. Umm Salama replied: I am from the people. See A.H. Abu Shaqqa, op. cit., p. 429.
27. In dealing with others, especially women, the Prophet has been described as 'the best of mankind in manners. He was not indecent in deeds or words. He was not making noise in the markets, nor he returned evil for evil but he excused and pardoned. He was neither rough nor harsh ... on the contrary, he was the softest and most kind of the mankind ... always cheerful and smiling. He used to patch his clothes and repair his shoes. He did not beat a servant or a woman; nor he struck anything with his hand except when fighting in the path of Allah. He was never asked for a thing; to which he said: No'. See Ibn Sa'ad, *al-Tabaqat*, Vol. 1, translated by S. Haq and H. Ghazanfar, *Pakistan Historical Society*, Karachi, Pakistan, 1967, pp. 422–33.
28. The influence of the Ansari women on the process of social change in the Medinan society was clearly illustrated by Umar who is reported to have said 'We, the people of Quraish, used to have authority over women, but when we came to live with the Ansaris, we noticed that the Ansari women

had the upperhand over their men, so our women started acquiring the habits of the Ansari women'. See *Bukhari*, op. cit., p. 388.

29. H.R. Ezzat, op. cit., pp. 106–15.

30. This view is also endorsed by the Board of Talimat-Islamiah – of the constituent Assembly of Pakistan. According to the Board, 'The idea of placing the burden of extra-domestic activities upon the shoulders of women at the expense of or in addition to the very important assignments which they are required to carry out in their own sphere of activity is repugnant to Islam and is not permissible except in times of extraordinary crisis and then too with many a limitation: participation in elections militates against many a requirement of Islam'. Cited in G.W. Choudhury, *Islam and the Modern World*, Scorpion Publishing, London, 1993, p. 55.

31. See, Mustafa al-Siba'i, *al-Mar'a Bayn al-Fiqh Wal qanun*, al-Maktab al-Islami, 6th edition, Beirut, 1984, pp. 151–3.

32. See *al-Ra'iy al-'Am*, 11 September 1996.

33. See *The Quran*, 4: 34, and 2: 228.

34. See H.R. Ezzat, op. cit., pp. 130–1.

35. See *Bukhari*, Vol. 1, pp. 181–2.

36. On these views, see *al-Ra'iy al-'Am*, op. cit., and Mustafa al-Siba'i, op. cit., pp. 40–1.

37. See *al-Ra'iy al-'Am*, 13 September 1996.

38. See H.R. Ezzat, op. cit., pp. 101–2. Also, see Abdul Halim Abu Shaqqa, op. cit., pp. 275–8.

39. Ibid., pp. 102–3.

40. See *Bukhari*, p. 819.

41. See *al-Ra'iy al-'Am*, op. cit. Also, al-Sebai, op. cit., pp. 39–40.

42. There are those who refuse to accept the *Hadith*, and argue that although it is narrated in Bukhari's Sahih, nevertheless, it is a fabricated *Hadith* and as such it has no legal bearings.

43. See M. al-Ghazali, *al-Sunnah al-Nabawiyya bayn Ahl al-Fiq wa Ahl al-Hadith*, Dar al-Shuruq, Cairo, 1989, pp. 48–50, C. Waddy, *Women in Muslim History*, op. cit., p. 33, D. Brown, *The Way of the Prophet*, Highway Press, London, 1962, pp. 110–11, and *The Quran* 27: 22–44.

44. The nature of the social life is illustrated by the statement of the second Caliph Umar which reads thus: 'We never used to give significance to ladies in the days of the pre-Islamic period of ignorance, but when Islam came and Allah mentioned their rights, we used to (acknowledge) their rights but did not allow them to interfere in our affairs'. See *Bukhari*, Vol. 7, p. 489.

45. H.R. Ezzat, op. cit., pp. 135–6

46. Ibid., pp. 137–40. Also, C. Waddy, op. cit., pp. 3–4.

47. The verse reads thus: 'Wives of the Prophet, you are not like other women. If you fear Allah, do not be too complaisant in your speech, least the lecherous-hearted should be moved with desire. Show discretion in what you say. Stay in your homes and do not display your finery as women used to do in the former days of *Jahiliyya*. Attend to your prayers, give alms to the poor, and obey Allah and His Apostle'.

48. H.R. Ezzat, op. cit., p. 141. Also, *Al-Mustakilah*, 8 April 1996.

Bibliography

The Quran: An English Translation of the Meaning of the Quran, Checked and Revised by Mahmmud Y. Zayid, Dar al-Choura, Beirut, 1980.

BOOKS

Al-Aqqad, A., *al-Mar'a Fi al-Quran al-Kareem* (Dar al-Hilal, Cairo, 1959).

Al-Arabi, I., *Ahkam al-Quran* (Dar, al-Kutub al-'Ilmiya, Beirut, 1988).

Al-Ati, H., *The Family Structure in Islam* (American Trust Publications, Indiana, 1977).

Al-Ati, H., *Islam in Focus* (American Trust Publications, Indiana, 1975).

Al-Asqlani, M., *al-Asaba* (Dar al-Kutub al-'llmiya, Beirut, 1995).

Al-Bukhari, *Summarised Sahih al-Bukhari* (Maktabat Dar-Us-Salam, Saudi Arabia, 1994).

Al-Faruqi, L., *Women, Muslim Society and Islam* (American Trust Publications, Indiana, 1988).

Al-Ghandur, A., *al-Ahwal al-Shakhsiyyah Fi al-Tashr' al-Islami* (Maktabat al-Falah, Kuwait, 1982).

Al-Ghazali, *Ihya Ulum al-Din* (Book 11, Sind Sagar Academy, Lahore, Pakistan, undated).

Al-Ghazali, M., *Qadaya al-Mar'a* (Dar al-Shuruq, Cairo, 1991).

Al-Ghazali, M., *al-Sunnah al-Nabawiyyah Bayn Ahl al-Fiq Wa Ahl al-Hadith* (Dar al-Shuruq, Cairo, 1989).

Al-Hatimy, S.A., *Women in Islam: A Comparative Study* (Islamic Publications Ltd, Lahore, Pakistan, 1993).

Al-Siba'i, M., *al-Mar'a Bayn al-Fiqh Wal-Qanun* (al-Maktab al-Islami, Beirut, Damascus, 1962).

Al-Tabari, Ibn Jarier, *Jami al-Bayan an Ta'wil al-Quran* (al-Halabi and Sons, Egypt, 2nd edition, 1954).

Al-Torki, S., *Women in Saudi Arabia: Ideology and Behaviour among the Elite* (Columbia University Press, New York, 1986).

Al-Turabi, H., *Women in Islam and Muslim Society* (Milestones, London, 1991).

Abdul-Rauf, M., *The Islamic View of Women and the Family* (Robert Speller and Sons, New York, 1977).

Abdul-Rauf, M., *Marriage in Islam* (Exposition Press, New York, 1981).

Abduh, M., *al-Mar'a Fi al-Islam* (Kitab al-Hilal, 1979).

Abd, M.Y., *Qadaya al-Mar'a Fi Surat al-Nisa* (Dar al-Dawah, Kuwait, 1985).

Abott, N., *Two Queens of Baghdad* (al-Saqi Books, London, 1986).

Adamu, M., *The Islamic Notion of Marriage and Divorce* (Joeart Productions, Laranto, Nigeria, 1987).

Ahmad, A., *Women and Social Justice* (Institute of Policy Studies, Islamabad, Pakistan, 1991).

Ahmed, L., *Women and Gender in Islam* (Yale University Press, New Haven and London, 1992).

Ail, P., *Status of Women in the Muslim World* (Aziz Publication, Lahore, Pakistan, 1975).

Alwan, A., *The Education of Children in Islam* (Assalam Press, Cairo, 1983).

Amarah, M., *Is Islam the Solution? Why and How?* (Dar al-Shuruq, Cairo, 1995).

Azad, A.K., *The Tarjuman al-Quran* (Edited and translated by Syed Abdul Latif, Kazi Publications, Lahore, Pakistan, 1930).

Badawi, J., *The Status of Women in Islam* (Gassin, Saudi Arabia, 1991).

Badawi, J., *Polygamy in Islamic Law* (American Trust Publications, Indiana, 1976).

Baveja, M.R., *Women in Islam* (Advent Books, New York, 1981).

Brown, D., *The Way of the Prophet* (Highway Press, London, 1962).

Chodkiewicz, M., *Le Sceau des Saints* (Gallimard, Paris, 1986).

Choudhury, G., *Islam and the Modern World* (Scorpion Publishing Ltd, London, 1993).

Cloudsley, A., *Women of Omdurman, Life, Love and the Cult of Virginity* (Ethnographica, London, 1983).

Coulson, N., *A History of Islamic Law* (Edinburgh University Press, Edinburgh, 1964).

Dearden, A., *Arab Women* (Minority Rights Group, London, 1983).

Doi, A.R., *Women in Shariah* (Ta-Ha Publishers Ltd, London, 1989).

Dorkenoo, E., *Cutting the Rose, Female Genital Mutilation: The Practice and its Prevention* (Minority Rights Publications, London, 1994).

Dorkenoo, E. and Elworthy, S., *Female Genital Mutilation: Proposals for Change* (Minority Rights Group, London, 1992).

El-Dareer, A., *Women, Why do You Weep?* (Zed Press, London, 1982).

El-Saadawi, N., *The Hidden Face of Eve: Women in the Arab World* (Zed Books, London, 1980).

Engineer, A.A., *The Rights of Women in Islam* (C. Hurst and Company, London, 1992).

Ezzat, H., *Women and Political Action: An Islamic Perspective* (The International Institute of Islamic Thought, Virginia, 1995).

Ezzati, A., *An Introduction to Shi'i Islamic Law and Jurisprudence* (Ashraf Press, Lahore, Pakistan, 1976).

Glasse, Cyril, *A Concise Encyclopaedia of Islam* (Cyril Glasse, ed. Stacey International, London, 1989).

Gulick, R., *Muhammad: The Educator* (Institute of Islamic Culture, Lahore, Pakistan, 1969).

Haeri, S., *Law of Desire: Temporary Marriage in Iran* (Tauris and Co Ltd, London, 1989).

Hamid, A., *Islam the Natural Way* (Muslim Education and Literary Services, London, 1989).

Hughes, T., *Dictionary of Islam* (W.H. Allen and Co, London, 1935).

Hicks, E., *Infibulation: Female Mutilation in Islamic North Eastern Africa* (Transaction Publishers, New Brunswick, New Jersey, US, 1993).

Ibn Kathir, *Tafsir* (Dar al-Qalam, Beirut, 1986).

Ibn Sa'd, *Kitab al-Tabaqat* (Dar Sadir, Beirut, 1980).

Ingrams, D., *The Awakened: Women in Iraq* (Third World Center, London, 1983).

Iwai, H., *Islamic Society and Women in Islam* (The Institute of Middle East Studies, International University of Japan, Japan, 1985).

Khadduri, M., *Islamic Jurisprudence* (The Johns Hopkins University Press, Baltimore, 1961).

Khan, Q., *Status of Women in Islam* (Islamic Book Foundation, Lahore/Washington, 1988).

Koso-Thomas, O., *The Circumcision of Women: A Strategy for Eradication* (Zed Books, London, 1987).

Jones, B. and V.R., *Women in Islam* (Lucknow Publishing House, Lucknow, 1941).

Jung, A., *The Muslim Law of Marriage* (Law Publishing Company, Lahore, Pakistan, 1978).

Levy, R., *The Social Structure of Islam* (Cambridge University Press, Cambridge, 1965).

Levy, R., *An Introduction to the Sociology of Islam* (Williams and Norgat Ltd, London, Vol. 1, 1931).

Makdisi, G., *The Rise of Colleges: Institutions of Learning in Islam and the West* (Edinburgh University Press, Edinburgh, 1981).

Malik, F., *Wives of the Prophet* (S.H. Muhammad Ashraf, Lahore, Pakistan, 1979).

Mawdudi, S.A.A., *Purdah and the Status of Woman in Islam* (Islamic Publication Ltd, Lahore, Pakistan).

Mawdudi, S.A.A., *The Law of Marriage and Divorce in Islam* (Islamic Book Publishers, Kuwait, 2nd edition, 1993).

Meinardus, O., *Christian Egypt: Faith and Life* (The American University Press, Cairo, 1970).

Mernissi, F., *Beyond the Veil* (al-Saqi Books, London, 1985).

Minai, N., *Women in Islam: Tradition and Transition in the Middle East* (John Murray, London, 1981).

Minces, J., *The House of Obedience* (Zed Press, London, 1982).

Mogannam, M., *The Arab Women* (Tonbridge Printer Ltd, London, 1937).

Murata, S., *The Tao of Islam* (State University of New York Press, New York, 1992).

Nasir, J., *The Status of Women Under Islamic Law* (Graham and Trotman, London, 1990).

Qutb, M.A., *Banat al-Nabi* (Dar al-Qalam, Beirut, no date stated).

Qutb, S., *Fi Zilal al-Quran* (Dar al-Shuruq, Beirut/Cairo, 1987).

Rahman, F., *Muhammad: Blessing for Mankind* (the Muslim Schools' Trust, London, 1977).

Rahim, A., *Muhammadan Jurisprudence* (Indus Publications, Lahore, Pakistan, 1968).

Rao, K., *Muhammad: The Prophet of Islam* (Islamic Propagation Centre International, United Kingdom, 1985).

Sabiq, A., *Fiqh al-Sunnah* (Dar al-Kitab al-Arabi, Beirut, 1977).

Sabiq, A., *Fiqh al-Sunnah* (Dar al-Fikr, Beirut, 1992).

Saeed, S., *Islam: From Revelation to Realization* (National Hijra Council, Pakistan, 1986).

Saqib, G.N., *Modernization of Muslim Education in Egypt, Pakistan, and Turkey: A Comparative Study* (Islamic Book Service, Lahore, Pakistan, 1983).

Saud, A., *Qatari Women: Past and Present* (Longman, London, 1984).

Schleifer, A., *Motherhood in Islam* (The Islamic Academy, Cambridge, 1986).

Shalaby, A., *History of Muslim Education* (Dar al-Kashshaf, Beirut, 1954).

Shukri, A., *Muhammadan Law of Marriage and Divorce* (AMS Press, New York, 1966).
Siddiqi, M.M., *Women in Islam* (Adam Publishers and Distributors, New Delhi, India, 1988).
Siddique, K., *The Struggles of Muslim Women* (Singapore, 1988).
Siddiqi, M., *Hadith Literature* (Islamic Texts Society, Cambridge, 1993).
Shaqqa, A., *The Liberation of Women at the Time of the Prophecy* (in Arabic) (Dar al-Qalam, Kuwait, 1994).
Szyliowi, J., *Education and Modernization in the Middle East* (Cornell University Press, Ithaca and London, 1973).
Tritton, A., *Materials on Muslim Education in the Middle East* (Luzac and Co. Ltd, London, 1957).
Ulama, M., *The Pious Women* (Young Men's Muslim Association, Port Elizabeth, South Africa, 1992).
United Nations. *The Worlds' Women: Trends and Statistics*, New York, 1995.
Waddy, C., *Women in the Muslim History* (Longman, London and New York, 1980).
Wasti, S.R., *Syed Ameer Ail on Islamic History and Culture* (People's Publishing House, Lahore, 1968).
Watt, M., *Muhammad at Mecca* (Oxford University Press, Oxford, 1979).
Watt, M., *Muhammad at Medina* (Oxford University Press, Oxford, 1988).
Westermarch, E., *The History of Human Marriage* (Macmillan and Co Ltd, London, 1925).
Zaitoun, L., *Questions and Answers About Women's Rights in Islam* (World Assembly of Muslim Youth, Saudi Arabia, no date stated).

CHAPTERS IN BOOKS

Al-Faruqi, L., 'Women in A Quranic Society', in Tesbah, H., Bahonar, M., and al-Faruqi, L., *Status of Women in Islam* (Islamic Propagation Organisation, Tehran, 1985).
Al-Sanabary, N., 'Continuity and Change in Women's Education', in Fernea, E., *Women and the Family in the Middle East: New Voices of Change* (University of Texas, US, 1985).
Afshar, H., 'Women, Marriage and the State in Iran', in Afshar, H., *Women, State and Ideology* (Macmillan, London, 1987).
Allaghi, F. and Almana, A., 'Survey of Research on Women in the Arab Gulf Region', in *Social Science Research and Women in the Arab World* (Frances Pinter, London and Dover, UNESCO, Paris, 1984).
Badawi, J., 'Women in Islam', in Ahmed, K., *Islam: Its Meaning and Message* (The Islamic Foundation, Leicester, 1980).
Badawi, L., 'Islam', in Holm, J. and Bowker, J., *Women in Religion* (Pinter Publishers, London, 1994).
Chishti, S., 'Female Spirituality in Islam', in Nasr, S., *Islamic Spirituality* (Routledge and Kegan Paul, London, 1987).
Dorph, K., 'Islamic Law in Contemporary North Africa: A Study of the Laws of Divorce in the Maghreb', in al-Hibri A., *Women and Islam* (Pergamon Press, London, 1982).

Gerner, D., 'Roles in Transition: The Evolving Position of Women in Arab-Islamic Countries', in Hussein, F., *Muslim Women* (Croom Helm, London, 1983).

Lemu, A., 'Women in Islam', in *Reading in Islam* (Malaysia, 1979).

McDermott, A., 'Saudi Arabia', in Dearden, A., *Arab Women* (Minority Rights Group, London, 1983).

Nasr, S., 'Islamic Education and Science', in Haddad, Y., Haines, B., and Findly, E., *The Islamic Impact* (Syracuse University Press, US, 1984).

Sanasarian, E., 'Political Activism and Islamic Identity in Iran', in Iglitzin, L. and Ross, R., *Women in the World* (Santa Barbara, California, 1986).

Smith, J., 'The Experience of Muslim Women', in Haddad, Y, Haines B. and Findly, E., *The Islamic Impact* (Syracuse University Press, US, 1984).

Stowasser, B.F., 'The Status of Women in Early Islam', in Hussein, F., Muslim Women (Croom Helm, London, 1983).

Tantawi, M., 'In the Shadow of the Quran', in al-Ghazali, M., Tantawi, M. and Hashim, A., *Women in Islam* (Dar al-Akhbar, Cairo, 1991).

Yamani, M. 'Some observations on women in Saudi Arabia', in Yamani, M. (ed.), *Feminism and Islam: Legal and Literary Perspective*, Ithaca Press, Reading, 1997.

JOURNAL ARTICLES

Al-Faruqi, L., 'Islam and Human Rights', *The Islamic Quarterly*, Vol. XXVII, No. 3, 1983.

Al-Faruqi, L., 'Islamic Traditions and the Feminist Movement: Confrontation Or Cooperation?', *The Islamic Quarterly*, Vol. XXVII, No. 3, 1983.

Adeleye, M.O., 'Islam and Education', *The Islamic Quarterly*, Vol. XXVII, No. 1, 1983.

Ajetunmobi, M., 'The Concept of Kuhla and Examination of Its Cases in Nigerian Courts of Shariah Jurisdiction', *Islam and the Modern Age*, Vol. XIX, No. 4, 1988.

Anees, M., and Athar, A., 'Studies on Islamic Education: An Interpretive Essay', *The Islamic Quarterly*, Vols XX and XXII, No. 4, 1978.

Diop, D., 'Tackling the Problem', *Health*, 26 April 2 May, 1993.

Esposito, J.L., 'The Changing Role of Muslim Women', *Islam and the Modern Age*, Vol. IV, No. 3, 1973.

Esposito, J., 'The Changing Role of Muslim Women', *Islam and the Modern Age*, Vol. VII, No. 1, 1976.

Hamidullah, M., 'Educational System in the Time of the Prophet', *The Islamic Culture*, Vol. 13, No. 1, 1939.

Mujahid, G., 'Education of Girls in Saudi Arabia', *Muslim Education Quarterly*, Vol. 4, No. 3, 1987.

Qayyum, S., 'Women in West Asia: A Case Study of Egypt', *Islam and the Modern Age*, Vol. IV, No. 3, 1973.

Qrunbum, A., 'The Political Economy of Infibulation', in *Journal for Sudanese Studies*, Khartoum University Press, Sudan, 1991.

Saeed, S., 'The Legal Status of Muslim Women', *The Islamic Quarterly*, Vol. XXIV, No. 1 and 2, 1980.

PERIODICALS

Al-Mustakilah.
Al-Ra'iy al-'Am.
Forward.
The Guardian.
Q-News.
The Times.
Reading Islam.

PhD and MA Dissertations

Al-Oteiby, M., The Participation of Women in the Labour Force of Saudi Arabia (North Texas State University, Denton, US, 1982).
Hallawani, E., Working Women in Saudi Arabia: Problems and Solutions (Claremont Graduate School, US, 1982).
Rehemi, M., A Survey of the Attitudes of Saudi Men and Women Toward Saudi Female Participation in Saudi Arabian Development (University of Colorado, US, 1983).

CONFERENCE PAPERS

Al-Deeb, S., 'To Mutilate in the Name of Jehovah or Allah, Legitimisation of Male and Female Circumcision', Unpublished Research, Institute of Canon Law, University of Human Sciences, Strasburg, France, 1994.
Khan, S., 'Understanding of Islam and Its Notions', Paper presented at the Euro-Islam Conference, Stockholm, June, 1995.

Index

Index